GURUS REDISCOVERED

Intercultural Research Series of Anthropography No. 2

GURUS REDISCOVERED:

Biographies of Sai Baba of Shirdi and Upasni Maharaj of Sakori

KEVIN R.D. SHEPHERD

Anthropographia Publications
Cambridge

First published in 1986
by Anthropographia Publications,
P.O. Box 13, Cambridge CB4 1EZ.

ISBN 0 9508680 2 7

Printed and bound in Great Britain by
Redwood Burn, Limited, Trowbridge, Wiltshire

CONTENTS

PREFACE

The two biographies comprising this book were first drafted in 1967. I rewrote them in 1978, using data hitherto unknown to me. I have more recently revised and added to them in accordance with anthropographic standards. The treatment will be found to differ very markedly from that of former versions in print, particularly in respect of Sai Baba of Shirdi. Anthropography stresses historical accuracy, and I have been at pains to assess what did actually occur, as distinct from what is popularly imagined to have happened.

At the same time, anthropography also stresses the quality of meaning and evolutionary potential in exceptional events. Due focus is therefore given to psychological features of these case histories that might normally be neglected in conventional historical analysis. I do not claim to have adequately depicted such features in their entirety, since I do not myself believe that these are entirely recoverable via the written word.

Kevin R.D. Shepherd

Intercultural Research Centre of Anthropography,
Cambridge

June 1985

PART ONE:

HAZRAT SAI BABA OF SHIRDI

CHAPTER ONE

THE BACKGROUND

Sai Baba of Shirdi died in 1918 at a village in the Deccan, an area of India subsequently given the official name of Maharashtra. He posthumously gained a wide celebrity in Western India, and also in other parts of the subcontinent. The popular image of him is that of a miracle-worker. One legend has it that he was not born of mortal parents, and emerged supernaturally into the world. (1) More critical investigators are under no obligation to believe this, particularly since the accumulating hagiography is contradicted by other extant source material. As often happens in relation to saints and others of kindred categories, devotees prefer substitute theories in place of more demanding data. Without wishing to cause any offence, it should be pointed out that fabulation amounts to a diminution of the true greatness of exceptional individuals.

During his lifetime Sai Baba was revered by both Muslims and Hindus as one of the greatest saints of the time. After his death he was increasingly elevated to the status of an *avatar*, meaning an incarnation of deity. This was the contribution of the Hindu following, the Muslim minority being eclipsed as an effective social mouthpiece. The role of *avatar* is a very common attribution and assumption in India, and in general can be regarded as a stock feature of sectarian rivalry amongst Hindu sects. However, some of Sai Baba's latter day following have a grievance with which it is easy to sympathize. This relates to the claims made for a certain namesake of the original Sai Baba, who encourages an obsession with wonder-working and is believed to be the avataric reincarnation of the Shirdi saint. (2) The more critical Hindus deem this sort of occurrence to be amusingly theatrical, but it is more serious when historical studies are affected adversely by popular gullibility. The fact is that some devotees view the original entity in the light of the nominal sequel, which is not the best method of historical inquiry.

The preoccupation with *siddhis* (occult powers) is one of the most infantile features of popular religion in India, and also in the West. It was specifically decried and warned against by such Hindu saints of calibre as Ramakrishna of Dakshineswar (d.1886) and his disciple Swami Vivekananda, (3) and also by the more recent Ramana Maharshi (d.1950). (4) The reasons for fostering such a preoccupation as a substitute for psychological development are obvious enough. Status accrues more quickly, and commercial interests are served by pandering to a credulous audience, particularly via the modern mass media.

Western readership has hitherto been largely dependent upon the biography of the Shirdi adept by Arthur Osborne. But in that book Osborne unfortunately lacked the personal acquaintance that distinguishes his writings on Ramana Maharshi. He was instead dependent upon devotee sources for his account, (5) and made exclusive use of the most well known (in India) but historically unreliable version of Sai Baba.

The person who was initially responsible for the literary casting of the figure in question was one Swami B.V. Narasimhaswami. He had never met Sai Baba, and came upon the scene in the 1930's, long after the saint's death. He compiled a three volume work entitled *Devotees' Experiences of Sai Baba*, along with a smaller work called *Sri Sai Baba's Charters and Sayings*. These books proved extremely influential. Many devotees accepted the contents uncritically, and they came to be regarded as the standard interpretation of the saint by the burgeoning Shirdi revival, which seems an apt description for the new wave of enthusiasm which centred upon the tomb and relics at Shirdi. In the pages of Narasimhaswami, Sai Baba is the wonder-worker who grants the wishes of his devotees. Narasimhaswami himself gained high esteem as a holy man within the movement he shaped as its leading spokesman. (6)

Comparatively few know about the events which led up to Narasimhaswami's debut as the expositor of Sai Baba.

An extant diary reveals that prior to his association with Shirdi, he approached Meher Baba at the latter's Nasik ashram with the request to stay with this Parsi ascetic. It was not easy to gain residence in Meher Baba's ashram, and as a suitable enticement for entry, the candidate offered to write Meher Baba's biography. The visitor was greatly offended to find that this Parsi, who observed silence, did not seem at all flattered by his proposal. Instead Meher Baba sent him away, adroitly suggesting that he write the biography of Upasni Maharaj, whom some regarded as the leading disciple of Sai Baba. Swami Narasimhaswami appears to have been one of those pundits who wish to write a successful book about a famous guru and accordingly be acknowledged as a prominent disciple of the guru. He duly presented himself before Upasni, who allowed him to stay at Sakori ashram, not far from Shirdi. Upasni appears to have permitted him free rein to express his talents, and the result was a glowing biography *The Sage of Sakori*, in which his own interpretations of events featured strongly. Meher Baba's subsequent comment on this biography was perhaps charitable: "Half of it is good and half of it absolute nonsense." The author rushed ahead with publication, but in the hour of his success, intellectual indigestion overcame him. Upasni was not always obliging in the way of doing exactly what his admirers expected of him, and Narasimhaswami found that he could no longer "accept" the guru he had so recently praised. Zeal deserted him, and he retreated from Sakori, regretting that he had wasted the flourishes of his pen.

In search of more amenable pastures, he moved to nearby Shirdi, drawn by tales of Sai Baba, who was conveniently dead and hence very predictable in his policies. Many of the disciples of the deceased had also expired, but to his delight he found that the local people, and also devotees living elsewhere, had a prodigious fund of memories concerning the saint. Many reminiscences were of a miraculous nature, which Narasimhaswami found particularly alluring. Here was his opportunity to write a book which would offset his former error. His penchant for stories of the miraculous was already evident in his biography of Upasni, but now he had much more scope for such description. He fastened upon tales of how Sai Baba's blessings caused barren women to beget the children they desired, how he lit lamps with water, how he placed his hand on the head of a poor man who consequently became rich, and so forth. Meher Baba later referred to these stories as "petty things." (7) This evaluation is the more convincing in view of the fact that Meher Baba had met the Shirdi adept personally, and because one of his closest disciples, namely Gustadji Hansotia, (8) had also been a close disciple of Sai Baba during the last several years of the latter's life. Meher Baba is only known to have encountered Sai Baba on one occasion, but owing to his close contact with Upasni Maharaj and others, he can be regarded on this account alone to have been much better informed than many of the devotees named in Narasimhaswami's records.

Instigating a widespread publicity programme for his new books, Swami Narasimhaswami was gratified at the response. People began to flock towards the shrine at Shirdi from all over India, very often in the hope of achieving some miraculous benefit. It was but a short step to commercialization. Shops did a booming trade in Sai Baba busts and calendars, and even matchboxes appeared emblazoned with the popularized image. There was certainly some truth in the claim that the name of Sai Baba had become almost a household word in India. Swami Narasimhaswami was indeed successful in that he himself became worshipped as a guru, (9) but an objective evaluation of his contribution is in general long overdue. Though he did salvage some interesting material, his editing favoured reports that buttressed the image of the wonder-worker, and the biographical details of Sai Baba's life suffered accordingly.

Amongst the subsequent books on the subject, (10) the best is that by Osborne. The Westerner sensed that Sai Baba had not been just one more of the mediocre gurus who play on popular sentiments. Singular methods, if haphazardly reported, distinguished him from mediocrity. Osborne's book was food for thought to Westerners who had never read of such an unorthodox "saint" before. But his attempt to distil the essence of the phenomenon was handicapped by Narasimhaswami's legacy, which provided his source of information. He incorporated the "miracles" along with more essential details, and a due reserve is called for. The only source acknowledged by Osborne is Narasimhaswami; he shows no knowledge even of Upasni Maharaj, let alone other important contacts of Sai Baba. But then, such extensions of the situation were not in favour with Narasimhaswami and other devotees. A dead teacher is much easier to follow than a living specimen.

According to Osborne, "practically nothing is known of his (Sai Baba's) early years." This was an error, one encouraged by Narasimhaswami's editing or ignorance of the relevant data. Osborne also wrote: "It is fairly certain that he was born of a middle-class Brahmin family." (11) This statement can be very strongly contradicted. The assumption of a brahmin parentage reflects the desire of the Hindu majority in Sai Baba's following to give their figurehead the most respectable auspices possible in the light of religious tradition. A full twenty years before Osborne's endorsement of Narasimhaswami appeared, another Western writer had reported Sai Baba to be a Muslim. Charles Purdom was following the earlier oral stream of information that was current in the Deccan immediately after the Shirdi adept's demise. (12)

It seems fairly certain that Sai Baba was actually born of a Muslim family. A Muslim researcher who wrote a little known article on the Shirdi adept was able to cite a book that was eclipsed by the wave of enthusiasm for Narasimhaswami's report. Written in Marathi and entitled *Bhakta-Lilamrut*, this book was written by Das Ganu, a Hindu devotee of Sai Baba who had personally known the saint. This neglected acount informs that Sai Baba was born a Muslim, (13) a disclosure which is the more convincing in view of the fact that Das Ganu was very much in favour of his native religion. This bias towards Hindu salients is discernible in other features of his account of Sai Baba.

The tension between unreconciled Muslim and Hindu details did not completely die out in the popular preference for a Hindu saint. Proponents of the extremist "immaculate origin" theory have affirmed that there is no satisfactory answer to the question of Sai Baba's subscribing to this or that creed. The question of creed, i.e. Islam or Hinduism, is quite understandably described as superficial, (14) but this is not what is really implied by the data. In seeking to elaborate a supernatural context for Sai Baba's birth, it is arguable that devotees are attempting to superficially resolve the question of his religious origin. But what the data actually reveals is that Sai Baba's early affiliation was to the sufi tradition, which is not to be facilely equated with orthodox Islam. In the context of historical biography, it is very relevant as to which tradition he primarily originated from.

The problem for popular Indian assessment in respect of the sufi tradition has been the diverse nature of the latter. The sufi affiliation of Sai Baba discernibly relates to an unconventional minority who are seldom described with accuracy or insight. This minority requires to be distinguished from the popular dervish orders, (15) which long ago became heavily conditioned by conventional codes, as happens with most institutional movements. This, however, should not be taken as any repudiation of the better values preserved by some institutional movements, which vary considerably in quality.

According to Das Ganu, Sai Baba was born at Selu, a village in Jantur Pargana. This was in the dominions of the Nizam of Hyderabad, (16) a Muslim ruler who retained many traditional customs deriving from the Mughal era. But this report omits reference to an elusive entity mentioned by Narasimhaswami, who says that Sai Baba left home at the age of eight to follow a "Muslim faqir," though there are no further details of the latter apart from the information that he died after a few years. Osborne follows suit in adding that Sai Baba then joined a Hindu guru.

Reverting to Das Ganu, we find that he scrupulously refrains from mentioning any such non-Hindu mentor. It seems that this source opted in large part for oral traditions of the Hindu majority in Sai Baba's following, despite the concession to Muslim parentage. But Das Ganu is much more informative on the subject's early years than Osborne, who can only relate that Sai Baba would refer to his Hindu guru by the name of Venkusa, and that after the latter's death, the disciple moved to Shirdi. In defence of this blank report, Osborne even states: "It is obviously not necessary to know about his early life or training; if it had been he would have told us." (17) This can be disputed; one complexity is that Sai Baba appears to have told much more about his early life to some pupils than to others. Osborne quoted some of Sai Baba's figurative stories relating to "Venkusa," and it is apparent that much of his speech was cryptic and intended as illustration. This factor needs to be taken into consideration, since disparate reports were evidently one consequence of his reminiscences. But the fact remains that Das Ganu left a fairly substantial description of Sai Baba's relationship with "Venkusa," though it shows distinct traces of hagiography that were conceivably imparted by the Hindu oral stock rather than by Sai Baba himself.

According to Das Ganu, Sai Baba passed his early childhood in the area of Aurangabad, a city founded in the Mughal era. His Muslim parents were poor, and when his father died, his mother took to the mendicant life in order to survive. Her young son accompanied her, and when he was only five, they arrived at Shelwadi. (18) This village was the property of a brahmin named Gopalrao Deshmukh, who had the local reputation of a guru. In recognition of his humanitarian activities, the British government had gifted him with Shelwadi as his hereditary tenure. He was hospitable to passing travellers, whatever their religion, and offered shelter to the destitute mother and son. He singled out the boy, perceiving in him an unusual potential.

Das Ganu's record seems to skip seven years until the boy was twelve, at which time his mother died and Gopalrao assumed guardianship of him. Against this is Sai Baba's reported statement that: "After my faqir's death, his widow left me with Venkusa." (19) It is apparent that affiliation with a Muslim *faqir* could have occurred in the very sketchy interim; one cannot even leave out the possibility that Sai Baba's own father was a *faqir* of some kind. The Arabic word *faqir*, equivalent to the Persian word *dervish*, is used very loosely in India, and can refer to very diverse types of ascetic or mendicant. The literal meaning of *faqir* is "poor one," and intrinsically refers to a state of development that is void of distracting surfeits. Sai Baba's use of the word seems to have been highly original, and the common associations of motley Muslim and Hindu "holy men" are probably apt to be misleading here. Female faqirs (*faqirat*) also existed, though in much smaller numbers.

The household deity of Gopalrao Deshmukh was Venkatesha, honoured by his family in accordance with tradition. It is tempting to link the auspices of Venkatesha with the mystery name of "Venkusa," indicating the deification of Gopalrao in Sai Baba's allusive speech. But Das Ganu treats as fact what would appear to be a figurative item in Sai Baba's reminiscences: Gopalrao was blind as a consequence of piercing his eyes with an iron poker to keep out the sight of things inciting to lust and greed. It would certainly not be the first time that allegory was mistaken for fact.

Other details have a much more realistic quality of reporting that indicate a factual accuracy, however approximate. Himself a brahmin, Gopalrao had many brahmin pupils. They observed that their guru treated his young ward with special favour, and some of them began to deeply resent that a Muslim was gaining preferential treatment. To their caste pride, the favoured one was effectively an untouchable. Matters came to a climax when the most biased amongst these men of priestly pedigree decided upon the drastic recourse of murder. One day they followed Gopalrao and his young disciple into the jungle adjoining Shelwadi, which the two often frequented. The envious perhaps thought that the Muslim was gaining secret instruction that should be vouchsafed only to priests. The trackers discovered Gopalrao and his ward taking a siesta beneath a shady tree. One of the jealous brahmins then took his opportunity to hurl a large chunk of stone at the head of the unsuspecting youth. Sheer malevolence must have disturbed his aim, for the missile is reported to have hit the guru instead, though not fatally as it transpired.

This event understandably disturbed the young Muslim

disciple. Since his teacher was now suffering on account of him, he begged permission to leave Shelwadi. But Gopalrao waved aside this request, and is reported to have said: "I have this day decided upon you as my sole chargeman, and one day you will succeed to my spiritual heritage." These words are likely to have been embellished in oral circulation, but we need not doubt in which direction Gopalrao's favours inclined.

It is reported that the offender who threw the stone was taken ill soon afterwards and died. His relatives implored Gopalrao to restore this man to life, but he disclaimed the exercise of *siddhis* (occult powers) and instead suggested that "the Muslim boy" might be able to do something. The story goes that the youth took a little dust from the guru's feet and applied it to the corpse, with the consequence that the dead man began to breathe again. Leaving aside any possible symbolism, this episode appears to have undergone the elaboration typical of the thinking of those who revered Sai Baba as a miracle-worker. The story would gain a great deal in feasibility if the sick brahmin had never in fact died, but was merely ill. Notable is Gopalrao's dismissal of *siddhis*, which are an unnecessary fiction if the better forms of alternative medicine are practised in such instances.

Gopalrao repeatedly declared that he would soon be terminating his earthly existence. But nobody took this too seriously in view of his apparent health. One day he gathered his close pupils around him and simply stated that it was time for him to go. He then took his daily bath, following this up with the traditional brahmin performance of *sandhya* (prayers) and recitations from the *Bhagavad-Gita*. He gave a last discourse, and then abruptly expired, startling everyone. One is reminded of the early death of Swami Vivekananda, a reliably documented phenomenon which has all the characteristics of a carefully planned and controlled expiry. Of less certain factual relevance is the detail that Gopalrao bequeathed to Sai Baba his old and well worn clothing, which the recipient retailored into an ascetic robe and headgear. This may well have been one of Sai Baba's purely allusive reminiscences describing his inner inheritance from the guru. The dervish robe (whether patched or no) has long been a subject for abstruse references in sufi lore.

Soon after Gopalrao's death, the Muslim disciple departed from Shelwadi, accompanying the marriage party of a Muslim Patel bound for the small town of Shirdi. He was doubtless still unpopular amongst brahmin devotees, whose antipathies would no longer have been restrained by the presence of the guru. His education at Shelwadi certainly goes a long way towards explaining the extensive familiarity with the Hindu tradition that he later exhibited, an affinity quite exceptional amongst Muslims.

The youthful Sai Baba now reaped the anonymity of the more sincere ascetics in India. He lived as a *faqir*, and seems to have been extremely indrawn and largely aloof from human contact. According to Narasimhaswami, he lived very simply under a *neem* tree at Shirdi, sitting in its shade during the daytime, sleeping on the bare ground at night. He begged his food in the mendicant manner, and ate whatever the villagers felt inclined to give him. Nobody knew who he was. His tendency was always to blanket out his past. His original name of birth seems never to have been known.

His open air abode under a *neem* tree inevitably invites a comparison with Hazrat Babajan of Poona, (20) a female *faqir* of advanced age, who tended to cryptic speech like Sai Baba. It is not impossible that the two met at some unrecorded venue. Their lifestyles were certainly very similar.

There is no doubt that Babajan was senior in years to our subject, though it is by no means certain what his exact age was. One cannot rely for precision upon the estimate of his age as being "about sixteen" when he first came to Shirdi. Narasimhaswami fixed the year of this latter event at 1872, which may or may not be correct. But his actual date of birth has been calculated at 1856, on the basis of sequences given by Sai Baba and interpreted factually. (21) A person of Sai Baba's disposition cared nothing for birthdays. Eyewitness estimates of age are not always reliable, and though he may not have looked as youthful as the young Ramana Maharshi, it is as well not to be dogmatic over dates in relation to his early life.

The young *faqir* did not remain long at Shirdi, and soon travelled on. Narasimhaswami was not successful in gaining coverage of the ensuing phase. Das Ganu fills the vacuum only slightly. We learn that our *faqir* maintained an itinerant life until he came to a mountain in the area of Aurangabad. He retired into a cave here, leading a severely ascetic existence for some years. He had achieved a high state of consciousness, and was oblivious of bodily needs, to the extent that he went without food and water during this sojourn.

Das Ganu's report was clearly oriented to the idea that the influences upon the subject's life were Hindu. But also misleading was the coverage afforded by a little known Muslim writer, Abdul Karim (Ramju) Abdulla, who too briefly reported statements made by his teacher Meher Baba in 1952, during a special itinerary to the Aurangabad locale. (22) Meher Baba pinpointed the exact location of a cave used by the Shirdi adept, which was situated in the near vicinity of Khuldabad, a small town approximately twenty miles north-west of Aurangabad, details which tally well enough with Das Ganu's less precise geography. More extravagantly, Meher Baba stated that the master of Sai Baba was Hazrat Zarzarizarbaksha, a medieval sufi of the Deccan who had achieved local fame amongst Muslims. This at least is the name by which he was subsequently known to Islamic posterity, a name meaning "Giver of the Wealth of wealths." According to Meher Baba, the name by which this entity was known during his lifetime was Khwaja Muntajebuddin. Another of his more popular titles is that of Dulay-Mian, meaning the "esteemed bridegroom," denoting his reputed achievement of mystical union. Meher Baba indicated that this entity had gone much further than the stage of union however, and that he was no less than a *qutub*. One of the most abused words in popular Sufism is *qutub* (axis, pivot); the status attaching to it has often been appropriated for institutional purposes. There was no publicity attaching to Meher Baba's disclosures concerning Zarzarizarbaksha, but Abdulla gave the misleading impression that Sai Baba was the literal disciple of

Zarzarizarbaksha. The actual context of Meher Baba's reference to these two Muslim entities was one of a reincarnatory link, i.e., Sai Baba was allegedly a disciple of Zarzarizarbaksha in a former life. (23) This is of negligible value for nineteenth century history. It may, however, be relevant here that Khuldabad was a site of strong sufi associations; the shrine of Zarzarizarbaksha is situated on a hill in this locale. One might take it that Meher Baba had tapped something of the eclipsed Muslim repertory at Shirdi, which did not otherwise survive in face of the Shirdi "revival" associated with Swami Narasimhaswami. Meher Baba himself connected with the ascetic ingredients of Sai Baba's Shirdi milieu; his close disciple Gustadji Hansotia (a Zoroastrian) had been one of the more ascetic pupils of Sai Baba, and inevitably in closer contact than householders with the floating population of Muslim ascetics who visited Shirdi.

The study of Sufism in the Indian subcontinent usually focusses upon North India, and comparatively little coverage is available for other regions. Yet the Deccan is one such region where a complex array of "sufi" trends were in existence for some centuries, coexistent with the various Islamic kingdoms established here since medieval times. The more obvious developments of interest in the north have largely eclipsed sufi history at places like Aurangabad, Khuldabad, Hyderabad, Ahmednagar, and Bijapur.

When Meher Baba in 1952 showed a select group of his pupils the cave used by Sai Baba in the Khuldabad locale, past ways of life were even then changing rapidly at urban level. Not only the era of the Muslim kingdoms, but also that of the British Empire, had faded into the past. Indian independence meant a renaissance of the Hindu spirit, and Indian ingredients attaching to the Muslim occupation have achieved a lesser degree of exposure. Reconstruction of relevant sufi events is not one involving religious insularity, as the case of Sai Baba so abundantly proves.

The small and peaceful town of Khuldabad, though currently insignificant in the urban sense, can boast a location rich in historical associations. Nearby, within easy walking distance, are the famous Rock Temples of Elluru, a major cave-complex which developed over many centuries and was used at different times by Buddhists, Jains, and Hindus. The origins of this temple site are thought to have been pre-Buddhist, though the most famous of its architectural achievements dates from the eighth century A.D. This is the Kailas temple of Shiva, an edifice carved out of the hillside rock with the most elaborate skill. This creation of master craftsmen was instigated at the period of the brahmanical revival when Buddhism was being superceded in India, its influence diminishing northwards, and ultimately to vanish from the land of its birth. British historians were formerly in the habit of assuming that "sacred activity" ceased in the region of Elluru in the wake of the general decline and decay of the cave-temples in medieval times. It is true enough that the old cave-complex became obsolete, but the closely adjacent activities of diverse sufis and dervishes should not pass unnoticed.

Ramju Abdulla reports an Islamic tradition of Western India which affirmed that, some centuries ago, the *awliya* or saints of Allah descended upon Khuldabad in 1,400 celestial palanquins. This legend preserves the distant memory of the extensive sufi infiltration of the area in the wake of the Islamic conquests here in the late thirteenth century.

Local mausoleums of princes and nobles provide some testimony to the regal splendour of the Islamic Deccan. But these have reaped comparative obscurity owing to the presence of sufi shrines, which are such a notable feature of the Khuldabad vicinity. According to Abdulla, there are more shrines of sufi saints and masters here than in any other similar rural township.

Amongst these shrines or dargahs is that of Shah Raju Quattal Husaini, the father of Sayed Muhammad ibn Yusuf al-Husaini (d.1422), alias Khwaja Banda Nawaz, though perhaps better known as Gesu Daraz. The latter was a *shaikh* of the Chishti order, and has the reputation of an "orthodox sufi" owing to his rebuttal of the teachings of Muhiyuddin ibn al-Arabi (d.1240), the Spanish Arab of heretical fame. Less well known is the fact that he denounced the Iranian sufi poets Fariduddin Attar (d.*c*.1225) and Jalaluddin Rumi (d.1273) as enemies of Islam. (24) This reflects the orthodox bigotry of some nominal sufis, who are more accurately to be described as Islamic theologians. Though he eventually settled at Gulbarga, another town in the Deccan, Gesu Daraz is linked with the early history of the Khuldabad locale owing to his early education in what the historian S.A.A. Rizvi describes as "the serene atmosphere of Daulatabad, which had been induced by many mystics who had gathered there." (25) His father had been forced to migrate to the city of Daulatabad (adjoining the Khuldabad vicinity), under pressure from the Turkish ruler of Delhi. The tension between the orthodox and the liberal Muslims was to continue in many guises.

Daulatabad was the Islamic name applied in the early fourteenth century to the Hindu city of Devagiri, which had fallen to the Turkish sultans. In 1326–7, Sultan Muhammad ibn Tughluq decided to make this city the second administrative capital of his empire, and forcibly imposed a migration to this location of a section of the Delhi elite. The migrants included *ulama* (doctors of the religious law) and sufi shaikhs, (26) though the latter were often synonymous with the former in the popular (and elitist) confusion of values attendant upon the term *sufi*. That there were many unorthodox sufi types in the later history of Daulatabad is not in doubt, though at urban level they may have been outnumbered by those who liked the atmosphere of the royal court rather than more humble rural environments. Ascetics made themselves scarce from the intrigues of power politics, since there were few rulers attentive to the betterment of their subjects, as was the Mughal emperor Akbar to an exceptional degree.

One of the most popular tombs at Khuldabad, reports Ramju Abdulla, was that of Sayed Zainuddin Shirazi, also known as Baviswen Khwaja or the "Twenty-second master." This appellation derived from the popular belief that twenty-one *murshids* (teachers) preceded him, transferring their spiritual dynamic to their successors through the medium of the robe (*pehran*) of the Prophet Muhammad. Abdulla reports that a garment purported to be this *pehran* was preserved at the tomb, but those critical of the relic mentality view this as an attribution of purely legendary associations. Stories of the prophet's *pehran* occur in relation to other lineages also. The idea of a spiritual transmission being bestowed by means of a physical object is incongruous in the deeper sufi perspective, which is much more difficult to perpetuate in popular terms.

Much legend has accrued to the tombs of Muslim saints in India. In the absence of recorded history, memories in oral circulation generally deteriorate into hagiography and crude local belief. No exception to this is the most famous of the Khuldabad dargahs, namely that of Hazrat Zarzarizarbaksha, a household word amongst Muslims of the Deccan according to Abdulla, who reported (in 1953) that over 10,000 people attended the annual pilgrimage to this shrine. This elusive entity is difficult to describe in reliable historical terms. One might well believe in such cases that truth is stranger than fiction.

Sai Baba may be considered a representative of the intrinsic aspect of the tradition sometimes known in India and Iran as *bi-shar*, which means "outside the law," i.e., the formal religious law maintained by the *ulama*. The contrasting term is *ba-shar* ("inside the law"), one often adopted by orthodox upholders of dervish orders, who insist upon such beliefs as "only a Muslim can be a sufi." The term *bi-shar* is very facile in common usage, and popularly refers to numerous sub-groupings affiliated to dervish orders, who at their worst were antinomian addicts of alcohol or hemp. It is easy to see why abuses of this kind were contrasted with the formal observance of Islamic customs, but the finer representatives of this unorthodoxy had very high standards which neither dogmatists nor perverts were able to meet.

What have been called *azad* (free) orders, (27) independent of the established variety, may be regarded as popular attempts to imitate the impact of entities like Sai Baba who are imperfectly remembered and interpreted. The principle of imitation often amounts to a sheer distortion. The crass intelligence of antinomian mystics invariably seeks to dilute the ascetic standards of those disciplined heretics who are unorthodox without being immoral.

In some respects, the intrinsic *bi-shar* tradition can be said to date back (at least) to Hallaj (d.922), the Arabo-Persian heretic who opposed the religious and bureaucratic elites of the Abbasid empire, forfeiting his life in the process. (28) Yet there were Hallajians of more orthodox associations like Fariduddin Attar, whose mystical writings have nonetheless annoyed dogmatists like Shaikh Gesu Daraz of Gulbarga.

Another discernible representative of *bi-shar* trends was Shams-i-Tabrizi, the thirteenth century teacher of Jalaluddin Rumi, and who is reported to have been murdered by the more orthodox amongst Rumi's "sufi" associates. However, it is as well to understand in relation to this episode that it was not so much orthodoxy but jealousy which was the motivating cause of this murder. (29) Nominal "sufis" seldom have anything worth being jealous of; like inferior mystics in general, they have very frequently assumed status which is of no more significance than being the cause of confusion in traditional and popular annals.

The word *sufi* has been devalued in common usage. It is evident that it originally signified a very rare psychological achievement, which is to be distinguished from many lesser states of mind. (30) Since Sai Baba appears never to have referred to himself as a sufi, I propose to credit him as one, in contradistinction to many bombastic mouthpieces who use this word vainly.

In order to help clarify such matters for those who find difficulty with basic facts, recent research on Bijapur is useful. This city of the Deccan is some distance south of Khuldabad, but many features of its history can be taken as being in general representative of Deccani trends as a whole. During the sixteenth century, Shia Islam was the "state religion" of Bijapur, and for the most part hostile to sufi trends. According to Eaton, the intellectual atmosphere of Bijapur "seems to have been remarkably sterile during most of the sixteenth century," the newly implemented doctrinal Shi'ism exerting a similar stifling influence to that which became the norm in Safavid Iran. Shia fanatics destroyed over two hundred Hindu temples during a campaign in Karnataka, and the monarch Ali I (rgd.1558–1580) was said to have personally smashed four to five thousand Hindu images. Many sufi types were emigrating to India from Iran at this time, but took care to avoid Bijapur. Yet all this changed with the new liberalism of Sultan Ibrahim II (rgd.1580–1627), which involved the ascendancy of a new political elite characterized as the more socially heterogenous and indigenous "Deccani class" which ousted the "conservative Foreigners," i.e. the Persian shi'is. Sunni Islam became the state religion, though the Sultan was not typically sunni in his policy of attempted reconciliation between Hindu and Muslim elements. This transition to tolerance resulted in a new wave of sufi types converging upon Bijapur. This contrasted dramatically with the situation then prevalent in Iran, where the monarch Shah Abbas I was sending to the executioners sufi types affiliated with both shi'i and sunni dervish orders. (31)

This Deccani counterpart of the Mughal liberalism in North India did not enjoy an unimpeded lease of life however. Many of the incoming "sufis," particularly those who were members of the Qadiri and Shattari orders, opposed the toleration as being religiously aberrant. Eaton has appropriately described them as "glorified *ulama*," and to their influence can in part be traced the orthodox reaction which stamped the reigns of the next two local monarchs. From fanatical Shi'ism the pendulum was now swinging to fanatical Sunnism, but with many of the dogmatic theologians finding it socially glamorous to be deemed sufis (a very common occurrence for centuries past, and still in vogue today). These latter insistently incited the court to strict Islamic orthodoxy, which was not in the interests of the subordinated Hindus. Some of these theologians accepted government land grants, a trend which created a "sufi petty gentry" in Bijapur. This gentry thrived on hereditary principles of continuation, and during the latter part of the seventeenth century some of these well-established "sufis" raised the cry of *jihad* (holy war) against the infidel, heedless of the sufferings of the non-Muslim population. Traditionalism is no guide to sufihood, though it is often an index to sheer unregenerate error.

The mentality of the courtiers and pedigreed "sufis" who invoked the *Quran* at all costs is reflected in such figures as Afzal Khan, who was despatched from Bijapur in 1659 at the head of 10,000 cavalry assembled to snuff out the Mahratta uprisings led by Shivaji. Afzal Khan can charitably be described as cruel – five years earlier he had threatened to have village officials "cut to pieces and squeezed in a mill" for failing to perform their duties. The famous episode in which Shivaji confronted Afzal Khan at Pratapgarh and killed him, has eclipsed the wanton destruction and desecration of Hindu temples by this military commander of Bijapur. While en route to fight Shivaji in the Western Ghats, he desecrated both the Tuljapur temple and the Pandharpur temple, destroying all the Hindu images he could find. Stories of his fanaticism spread swiftly throughout Maharashtra, and are thought to have spurred the Hindu retaliation. (32)

A loathing of a comparable kind must have been experienced by those Muslim ascetics who are known to have opted for a withdrawn existence in the face of the zealous "sufi" puritans who were eager to wield the sword and to urge its use. They were amongst the spectators as the other "sufis" profitably joined the landed class or opted for the enterprise of tomb-cults. Family descendants of reputed sufis would claim the inheritance of the spiritual powers of the latter, a sanctification of blood ties that was popularly accepted (and cultivated), and which endowed the descendants (*pirzadas*) with considerable social prestige. A fitting accompaniment to such crass opportunism was the concept of the saint's tomb as the physical repository of his *baraka* (blessing, vibratory quality). The *pirzadas* monopolized these tombs in the profitable manner typical of misrepresentation. They would freely make "disciples" (*murids*) of any illiterate willing to demonstrate his belief in the *barakat* (spirituality) of the favoured tomb. (33) It is no wonder that superstition and miracle legends became such a feature of tomb-cults. Such people had no intention of, and no comprehension of, implementing the authentic sufi principle of being selective in enrolling disciples on the basis of spiritual merit. Much the same can be said of the highly literate and pedigreed *ulama* who gained adulation and respect as purported sufis.

The "orthodox sufis" reserved some of their choice barbs for the unorthodox sufis and their disciples. The former caricatured the latter as "madmen" (*majazib*; singular: *majzub*), a blanket term which meant that they did not hate Hindus, did not bulwark pedigree and corrupt monarchy, did not sanction concealed motives for the appropriation of worldly benefits, did not hold forth in dogmatic and censorious tones against everything that happened to hinder the cause of status and exclusivist tradition. For their part, the *majazib* regarded the *ulama* type of sufi as fanatical predators, and were averse to the institutions of urban Islam – which included the dervish orders.

Large numbers of "majzubs" appear in the sources relevant to the late seventeenth century and early eighteenth century at Bijapur, a fact which can comprise a problem for generalizations which do not recognize differences amongst this grouping. The large numbers are interpretable in terms of the inevitable popularization attending such trends when reported in any detail. A wide variety of dispositions and backgrounds are evident in the composition of the *majzub* trend. Some of these "madmen" originated from noble families, some came from a career of government service, some were ex-military men, some were the sons of orthodox sufis (a number of them had respectable Chishti origins; the Chishtis were the least bigoted of the major orders in the Deccan, and preserved a stronger sense of asceticism). But they had renounced their privileged lifestyles, and in general were practically indistinguishable from commoners. Less socially privileged persons were also majzubs, but it is very difficult to trace their backgrounds. At the fringe (probably a large one) was an undisciplined element of hangers-on who were addicted to opium, *bhang*, and wine. They had much in common therefore with the less scintillating specimens amongst Hindu sadhus and yogis, who are notorious for their partiality to *bhang*. *Bhang* is a narcotic prepared from the leaves of hemp; it was variously eaten, smoked, or drank. It was identified with the lower classes of the population, but the Muslim establishment of Bijapur rather conveniently associated the drug with nonconformists in general. The crux of the matter is that the *majzub* identified themselves with non-elite groups, in rejection of the policy of the orthodox sufis.

Though the information on them is piecemeal, it is evident that the majzubs forsook the trappings of conventional Sufism such as the *dargah* (tomb) and the *khanaqah* (retreats associated with the orders). They appear to have ignored the standardized dervish exercises associated with the *zikr* invocations, which had in any case become an extroverted substitute for self-recollection. Not only this, but they remained aloof from the outward observances of Islam, which had become a fetish of the worldly sufis. Some went about naked like Hindu sadhus, ignoring the taunts of the distinguished shaikhs who prided themselves upon their own decorous appearance as holy men.

None of the majzubs at Bijapur are known to have written books. Most sufi literature at that period followed a stereotyped pattern in imitation of the earlier "classical" phase, and was frequently produced by orthodox members of the dervish orders. The majzubs are described in hagiographies that frequently amount to a caricature of the subject. Typical entries on them merely state the name, place of origin, and some aspect of behaviour that "seemed particularly bizarre to the biographer," to borrow an apt phrase of Eaton. It is apparent that the more bizarre features of the trend led to cases of charlatanism; *murshids* in pursuit of glamour were not restricted to the ranks of the orthodox sufis. External characteristics are the easiest thing to imitate, though popular credence can seldom discern this.

Some of the Bijapur majzubs were persecuted by the social elite, doubtless on the pretext of their contempt for the outward observances of Islam. (34) The orthodox sufis had a vested interest in screening out ideals that conflicted with custom, even though their habits rendered them as ogres for both the unprivileged Muslims and the unprivileged Hindus.

The *majzub* phenomenon should not be viewed as something unique to Bijapur. On the contrary, there are indications that it was a widespread trend that was represented here, and one not to be chronologically contracted. For instance, the heretical Jewish sufi known as Sarmad (d.1660/1) was active in Delhi during the mid-seventeenth century, and was there castigated as a *majzub*. He had earlier sojourned at Hyderabad, and was notorious amongst the orthodox Muslims for his affinities with Hindu ascetics. Sarmad went naked in the manner of sadhus, but was a highly literate *majzub* who was learned in, amongst other branches of knowledge, the Arabic tradition of Peripatetic philosophy and Hebrew rabbinical literature. He was a rarity in frequenting court circles, but this was owing to his capacity as mentor of the liberal Mughal prince Dara Shikoh, who represented harmony between Muslims and Hindus. Both Shikoh and Sarmad were executed by their opponents, (35) but less politically prominent *majazib* ensured a survival of the unorthodox sufi tradition. In more modern times, this tradition has been represented by such figures as Sai Baba, Hazrat Babajan of Poona, and Tajuddin Baba of Nagpur. (36)

It is conceivable that the toleration which marked the policy of the Chishti order during the eighteenth century was a consequence of influence from the *majzub* tradition. Shah Kalimullah Jahanabadi (d.1729) of Delhi sent a Chishti disciple to Aurangabad, then the imperial camp of the Mughal emperor Aurangzeb, with instructions to "enrol disciples at all costs." Though part of an institutional programme, it was a remarkably broad-minded one, accepting both Shia Muslims and Hindus into the Chishti fold without converting them to Sunni Islam. (37) This duplicated the attitude of the non-institutional *majazib*, who were disdainful of protocol. It was also the attitude of the Kaivani school, named after the Zoroastrian *ishraqi* adept Azar Kaivan (d.1618), who emigrated from Iran to North India during the reign of Akbar. Kaivan and his Zoroastrian disciples were neutral in the sunni versus shia conflict, and made disciples of Muslims, Hindus, and Jews in their non-institutional activity. (38)

Sai Baba was doubtless one of those who took the view that since a large number of Muslim families had been converted from Hinduism, and had consequently retained

Hindu social customs for long after, it was additionally disruptive to emphasize religious differences like the orthodox sufis did. The Deccan was a particular focus for this type of Muslim heritage, at least at rural level.

The term *majzub* is interchangeable with other terms in signifying the trend under discussion. The literal meaning of the Arabic word *majzub* varies in different glossaries, but in general it signifies a sufi saint who becomes absorbed in Allah. In the Bijapur tradition, it referred to those who forsook Islamic orthodoxy in favour of an ascetic life in which states of consciousness (and not rites and customs) were the paramount consideration. The plural term *majazib* has appropriately been translated as "illuminati," (39) and this seems an apt description, in terms of sufi priorities and perceptions, for the tradition of which Sai Baba emerges as a distinctive representative. It is clear that much of this tradition has evaded academic research, particularly since it operated outside the dervish orders, to which most of the extant documents apply. In this unorthodox tradition, it is evident that discerning Hindus featured strongly, some of them becoming important disciples, and even successors, of sufi masters. Conversely, developing sufis of Muslim background would sometimes train under genuine Hindu adepts for a longer or shorter period. At public level, matters were often confused by the sham exponents in both these fields. Faqirs, sadhus, and yogis addicted to *bhang* and other sensational pastimes are only liable to mislead those of similar disposition, but if the public are indoctrinated with concepts of *siddhis* (occult powers), then they are open to deception at every moment.

It is known that Sai Baba had at least one mentor after Gopalrao's death, and his ascetic sojourn in the cave near Khuldabad may have been initiated by someone who escaped record. It is not going too far to infer tht the most important part of Sai Baba's training eluded the later annalists.

It is very feasible that Sai Baba's stay in the Khuldabad cave resembled that of his disciple Upasni Maharaj at a certain deserted temple near Shirdi, the main difference being that Sai Baba was much younger in years. However, considerations of age do not count for very much in the *majazib* tradition. The pious greybeards who aired their seniority amongst orthodox sufis were very often those displaying the most crass ignorance of sufi essentials.

The general ascetic milieu of Sai Baba was in many ways unchanged from that of earlier centuries in the Deccan. Bijapur and other Muslim kingdoms had fallen to the Mughal expansions, but during the eighteenth century, Nizam-ul-Mulk Asaf Jah had subsequently created the sprawling Muslim state which had its capital at Hyderabad. The Nizam of Hyderabad afterwards became an ally of the British, his government retaining a strong sense of Mughal customs. Khuldabad was situated on the periphery of the Nizam's territory, which was still officially Muslim soil. This situation existed until 1948, when the new government of independent India absorbed Hyderabad and partitioned it amongst the new linguistically-organized states of the Deccan. By that time Hyderabad state numbered seventeen million people, only fifteen per cent. of which were Muslims. (40) But until the mid-twentieth century, there was comparatively little change in rural life since the Mughal era.

In the 1870's the wave of Western education brought by the British had not yet reached the towns, only the major cities of the country. The Muslims were much more conservative than the Hindus in this respect, and for long they retreated into their traditional thought patterns. But a man like Sai Baba was equally aloof from both the British colonialists and the Muslim conservatives; both parties would have found it extremely difficult to understand the rationale of his existence.

In the Khuldabad cave, Sai Baba appears to have experienced the activation process associated with the *lataif*, the "subtle organs" of perception. The *lataif* process has been considered analogous to what is known to Hindus as *kundalini*, but it has been said that the *lataif* remain a mystery to the uninitiated whatever the presumed knowledge gained by acquaintance with tradition. There are also said to be dangers involved for the unprepared. Few modern enthusiasts seem to be aware that grave psychological imbalance can ensue from an unwise preoccupation with this subject. One wonders what the modern day expositors of "kundalini yoga" would do if their much advertised methods really worked, and they found that their swelling classes of paying students were suddenly rendered financially ineligible as a consequence of one or more of the varied physiological and psychological hazards of which bungling practitioners have been warned in grave terms by departed experts. Many persons on the "path" assume the role of teachers, when in fact they represent the worst danger to persons of small discernment. The activation process can be accidentally triggered by one of these callow exponents with diverse consequences of mishap. The activation process can only be successful under a highly qualified guidance, which is much rarer than popular standards will admit. Wrong activation can cause serious illness.

This activation process is rendered more complex by the two-fold occurrence of what is known in sufi terminology as *fana* (absorption) and *baqa* (permanence). These have become over-simplified terms in some literature; the two states of entity signified are often treated as ultimate achievements, but there are much lower conditions on the "path" to which this basic alternation can apply. The quality of *fana* and *baqa* therefore varies enormously, though all lesser degrees bear small comparison to the ultimate *fana* and the ultimate *baqa*. Suffice it to say here that Sai Baba appears to have undergone an intense *fana* at the Khuldabad cave, and was subsequently helped to achieve a due equilibrium in *baqa* involving the "normalization" of his consciousness in relation to the external world.

Typically enough, Das Ganu reports a Hindu adept at this juncture; Sai Baba is reported to have contacted the "renowned Swami of Akalcut." The details are very obscure, and there is perhaps no justification for assuming that no Muslim was involved. The factor of more than one guiding agency is attested in other case histories, though hagiographies are prone to a selective manipulation of details.

The next event recorded is that of Sai Baba's return to Shirdi. The entire phase which occurred between his two appearances at Shirdi is relegated to a single sentence in Osborne's recapitulation: "He wandered away again, roamed about for a while, and then came back and spent the rest of his life there." (41) Such is the historical fate of the higher evolution of consciousness in exceptional human beings.

According to Das Ganu, Sai Baba was twenty when he reappeared in Shirdi, but one suspects that this was a conveniently round number in retrospect. Estimates of the subject's age should be treated with caution as I have earlier observed. Osborne, working from an obvious dearth of material, proffered no such estimate of age, and no year date unlike the first occasion. But we can be quite sure that Sai Baba, at this early period, was no greybeard, no patriarchal being whose wisdom was measured by wrinkles. He was still a young man, and probably not in his prime. To the old men of Shirdi, and even to the middle-aged, he seemed very much a junior in appearance. But implications of the leap made in conscious range via the *fana-baqa* process are not contracted by surface appearances; with him, as with others much older than he, the gap in time crossed in terms of consciousness can be described as astronomical in relation to less developed time-sequences.

CHAPTER TWO

AT THE SHIRDI MOSQUE

Shirdi was one of those rural communities of India that could be termed a village or a small town depending upon how one defines either. Life had gone on here in exactly the same way for generations on end, and little was heard of the outside world. The population comprised a mixture of Hindus and Muslims, though the latter were a distinct minority. Geographically, Shirdi is some sixty miles west of Aurangabad, and about the same distance north of Ahmednagar. It was six miles from the nearest railway station of Kopargaon. There were no known associations of historical or spiritual importance in connection with the place.

When Sai Baba reappeared here, he at first lived in the open air under a *neem* tree. Very little is known of his early years at Shirdi, and it is clear that at least one incident later reported was a fabrication of the hagiographers. His earlier visit to Shirdi is credited with the following anecdote: when alighting from the cart that had been used to transport the marriage party from Shelwadi, one of the spectators shouted out "Welcome Sai!" (42) This story thus explained the origin of the saint's name, and in a laudatory context. But the current version of this story omits reference to the fact that it was a Muslim marriage party whom the young *faqir* was accompanying, and names a Hindu, one Mahalsapati, as the spectator who coined the name. In view of other events reported, it is extremely unlikely that this story is reliable, and it can be regarded as an invention of the Hindu majority at a much later date.

Sai is not a Hindu name, but a Persian word indicative of a holy man. It seems to bear an affinity with the Arabic *sa'ih*, which in the early medieval era of Islam was used to designate itinerant ascetics of sufi background. It appropriately reflects the Muslim background of the subject.

Though Swami Narasimhaswami insisted upon regarding Sai Baba as a Hindu, his own narrative affords ample proof to the contrary. One can deem reliable the episode reported of how, after his reappearance at Shirdi, the young *faqir* went to a small Hindu temple to take shelter. The custodian of this temple was Mahalsapati, the same Hindu abovementioned. Far from welcoming the stranger as a holy man, Mahalsapati refused him entry to the sacrosanct precincts, reserved for Hindus only. The reason for this is convincingly reported that Mahalsapati regarded the visitor as a Muslim *faqir*. The custodian told the rebuffed to go and live at the local mosque. Islamic territory could be the only place for him.

This realistic detail gains extra credence from the description of the Shirdi mosque as a very humble building that seems to have been much less commodious than the temple. It was a small mud-walled structure, a mosque of the distinctly provincial variety that would not bear comparison with the more ornate specimens to be found in the pages of tourist guides. It appears to have been no more than about fourteen feet square. It was in a dilapidated condition; the east side had no wall at all, and allowed a scant protection against the onslaught of wind and rain. Outside steps led up to the level of the plain earthen floor. Fronting the open side of the building was a compound entered by a gate set in the wall. The setting was bare and primitive. Here Sai Baba made his abode, spending the rest of his life as an occupant of this rural place of worship. Yet he did not function as any orthodox religious overseer; quite to the contrary in fact.

The reasons why the custodian of the Hindu temple regarded him as a Muslim are not difficult to ascertain. Apart from any question of appearance at this time (which largely escaped recording), he was heard to utter sacred phrases in Arabic and Persian, and sometimes repeated *namaz*, the ritualistic prayer of Islam which tradition decrees should be intoned five times a day. His observance of *namaz* was very irregular, and would have accordingly earned the disapproval of doctors of the law.

To the local people it was evident that he was a Muslim.

It was only much later when fame had accrued to him, that Hindus began to regard him as one of their own. At this early period however, even Narasimhaswami makes it clear that the local inhabitants were unintorested in him, regarding him merely as another holy man. They were respectful maybe, but no more.

He himself facilitated this non-interest by maintaining an unwavering aloofness. He spoke only when necessary, and was not at all amenable to casual conversation. His extremely taciturn demeanour was accepted, and nobody bothered him. He seemed eccentric in the general opinion, perhaps slightly crazy even. This is how people often interpret a lack of garrulousness.

Though carefully cultivating an unsociable air, there was yet evidence that he was not at all insensitive to the community around him. Occasionally, he would emerge from the mosque precincts upon special request in order to treat ailing people with his knowledge of herbal remedies and drugs. (43) In this, he was the equivalent of a local doctor, other medical facilities being non-existent in Shirdi at this date. This form of alternative medicine was not uncommon amongst sadhus and faqirs, though the skill in application varied prodigiously, to say the least.

In appearance he was tall and gaunt, moving with a lithe step. He seems to have spent most of his time in the mosque or adjoining compound, save for begging a handful of food. An unusual habit of his was to keep a fire constantly burning in the mosque. A *dhuni* or sacred fire is fairly common to Indian holy men, and though it is not an Islamic custom, faqirs have adopted it. To find this practice in a mosque, however, was extremely unorthodox, and more reminiscent to some of Zoroastrian fire temples. It could only have happened in such a rural setting.

Though he discouraged attention from the locals, there was one section of society with whom he did converse at intervals. These were the passing mendicants, both Hindu and Muslim, sadhus and faqirs, although these general divisions have comprised acute gradations in quality which were often lost upon superficial observers. The people of Shirdi were not much aware of these interchanges, until one of the wanderers told a local audience: "That young *faqir* is like a jewel on a dunghill."

Even then, nobody really uprated him. Intermittent, vaguely curious onlookers were quite unaware of significances to which they were not accustomed. One may take it that "dunghill" referred not only to the commonplace, battered mosque, but also to the unperceiving community in which the anonymous sufi had chosen to dwell. Dung, however, can become a useful commodity in the hands of a good gardener.

One of the unknown men who passed through Shirdi may have been the sufi who became known as Banemiyan Baba. This Muslim was one of the many lesser known saints of the Deccan during the early part of this century. It was Meher Baba who established Banemiyan's original identity as a disciple of Sai Baba; the same informant described Banemiyan as a *majzub*, (44) using this term in an unusual sense denoting a specific achievement of the ultimate *fana*. The implication of such terminology, in this instance, is that Banemiyan had not achieved the advanced *baqa* of Sai Baba. Such distinctions are rarely made in more popular channels of expression. Banemiyan's association with Sai Baba seems in general to have been entirely forgotten, if indeed it was ever known to more than a bare handful. One reason for this is that Banemiyan did not live at Shirdi, but at the city of Aurangabad.

One of the most frequently encountered notions about "masters" is that they have their closest disciples in their immediate proximity. This seems a very superficial convention. Sai Baba's perspective seems rather to have been equivalent to an elementary principle of superfluity, i.e., it does not need two electrical batteries to supply a circuit for which one alone is sufficient.

Another reason for such obscurity is the fact that it was many years before a widespread public fame accrued to Sai Baba. This did not occur until about 1900 or just after, and the two decades of his life at Shirdi prior to this date remain to a large extent hazy and undefined. It was only the concluding period that Narasimhaswami caught up with in any detail, and that very distortedly.

Long before the end of the century however, the Shirdi inhabitants themselves had come to accept Sai Baba's importance. The episode quoted by Narasimhaswami as the reason for this change of attitude is typical of the vulgarizing tendencies which this chronicler so eagerly promoted.

The taciturn *faqir* was in the habit of burning small oil lamps in his mosque, and occasionally requested a little fuel from the local shopkeepers. One day they refused him however, not because they deemed his request exorbitant, but because they were in the mood for diversion and wished to see the reaction of this very uncommunicative character. He did not react at all however, but merely turned around and retraced his steps. By this time a group of curious bystanders had accumulated, and at someone's suggestion the small crowd followed him back to the mosque, feeling entertained at the event in the manner characteristic of mob intelligence. The burning question of the day had now become: "What would he do now without his oil?" According to Narasimhaswami, the silent *faqir* picked up a pot of water, and filled his array of lamps from this receptacle. Setting light to them, they burned in the normal manner. The startled mob fell at his feet in awe, begging his forgiveness for their lack of respect.

Whatever it was that actually happened, the whole Shirdi community began to revere him as a consequence. The role of the mob element smacks of truth, and the *faqir* may well have deemed it time to give such loiterers a lesson. The feat reported is suited to the standards of mob intelligence, and one could well pause to reflect that Sai Baba was hardly likely to have delivered a glowing discourse on the intricacies of the sufi path, or on the poetic niceties of sufi literature. A mob is a mob, and requires to be kept under control by effective means. The irony here is that even if it were fact (even in the sense of a sleight of hand), the "miracle" of the lamps would be deemed child's play, and normally beneath contempt, by even the most partially developed sufi types. Narasimhaswami's mistake was (like the mob he reports) to dilate upon this and other peurile wonders as great and exciting events proving spiritual advancement.

There was very little Sai Baba could do with small minds limited to daily routines, other than provide the traditional form of medical treatment and thereby alleviate suffering. The social reassessment of him on the basis of incorrect criteria did nothing to alter his taciturnity in general. He did speak to those who approached him for counsel, but it was usually in a very cryptic fashion. He certainly did not start lecturing in the market-place. Instead, he seemed indifferent as to whether anybody knew of his existence or not.

So far he had been a completely nameless entity, but it was now that he gained his familiar cognomen. *Baba* (father) is a common title in India, and one of Islamic associations, but *Sai* is more pronouncedly in the Muslim idiom, denoting a saint.

The new social awareness of him did prompt a comparative minority to observe him more closely and to realize accordingly that he was not by any means an ordinary *faqir*. They wondered how these perceptions could possibly have escaped them previously. A group of pupils began to form, as distinct from the admirers who were lost in awe and reverence. It was evident to these new pupils that quality of attitude was the key to commencing any deep link with him.

One of these early Shirdi pupils was none other than the fastidious keeper of the Hindu temple who had once barred him admission to that aforementioned shrine. His name was Mahalsapati, and from his memory was later garnered the report of the only clearly dated incident of this lengthy period. It was during the year 1886 that Sai Baba told him: "I am going to Allah. Take care of this body for three days. If I return I will look after it myself. If not, bury it in that open land over there and put up two posts to mark the spot." After delivering this startling message, his breathing stopped and his heart ceased to beat. The civil authorities held an inquest and announced that Sai Baba had died, although they could not explain why. He was still in his prime apparently, and had been in good health. Mahalsapati was ordered to bury or cremate the body, in accordance with the Indian law prohibiting a corpse to be kept longer than twenty-four hours. But he did not forget the adept's injunction, and refused to carry out the contrary order, despite official exasperation. On the third day Sai Baba's abdomen was seen to move, and his breathing began again. Then he opened his eyes and returned to physical life as if nothing had happened.

There is no doubt that there were some strange episodes to Sai Baba's life, which tend to be unexplainable in terms of everyday perspectives. The problem is one of gaining due context; the pursuit of miraculous ingredients amounts to a loss of context in events that are of more than mundane significance.

His pupils learnt to expect the unusual, and had to adjust their ideas of adeptship. His teaching methods were certainly not the standard expository variety which frequently send people to sleep in one way or another. He rarely gave discourses, and visitors would wait in vain for wisdom to trip fluently from his lips in an easily assimilable form, perhaps not pausing to dwell on the well known fact that what goes in one ear quite often departs through the other.

He did not cater for any expectancy that would-be pupils might harbour. In fact, he sometimes seemed bent upon discouraging attention from them. He might even appear angered at disturbance, or make himself appear socially uncouth. Conventional etiquette was not the rule at the Shirdi mosque, where Sai Baba would cough and spit freely in the presence of visitors while smoking tobacco in a foul earthen pipe. This was particularly offputting to the more refined urban visitors who arrived in his later life, but he had other ways of making himself appear distasteful. All this accords with a time-honoured sufi technique for the purpose of ensuring that the casuals either go elsewhere or alter their approach.

Sai Baba would doubtless have expressed a rugged amusement at the contemporary notion then prevalent in both India and the West that holy men do not smoke. Swami Vivekananda was also partial to tobacco pipes, and met typical criticism in this vein from his more narrow-minded detractors. Both Vivekananda and Sai Baba of Shirdi can usefully be distinguished here from the category of sadhus who smoke hemp, a category who were evidently copied by some Muslims. Hemp-smokers tend to adopt a placid and starry-eyed demeanour that has fooled tyros into believing that the former are in a state of spiritual equipoise. By comparison with this suspension of the faculties, both Vivekananda and Sai Baba tended to an explosive and dynamic personality that often put paid to pet delusions. One could make a superficial case for the sterling qualities of tobacco, but one suspects that the inspiration was much deeper in these particular instances.

There have been many sufi teachers who have been noted authors of their day, and many others who have made use of special literature when the occasion demanded. There have been yet others who dissociated themselves from books, and Sai Baba was one of these. But this can be misleading if taken out of context. What he discouraged was not so much the act of reading, but the tendency to dogmatism and religious insularity that were such divisive features of his environment. Both Hindus and Muslims were apt to be proud of their textual heritage, and would accordingly blinker themselves with preconceptions. He is reported to have said: “People hope to find Brahma (God) in these books, but it is confusion and not Brahma that they find there.”

In some cases he would instruct a pupil to study a scriptural volume whose contents were suited to their development needs. In other cases he would discourage the reading of particular books, perhaps perceiving that no requirements of a psychological development would be met.

Sai Baba himself did not read books. At one period he had the *Quran* recited before him for about half an hour daily, while he sat with a group of attentive pupils. But he would not himself even touch the sacred book. For years some of his pupils wondered if he was illiterate in view of his distinctive avoidance of literature. It was difficult to tell from his speech the extent of his possible literacy. He was often heard to repeat sacred phrases in Arabic or Persian, but always in an undertone, as though he did not wish to be heard (possibly a consideration extended to his Hindu followers). When speaking in the local Marathi dialect, Islamic terms tended to emerge. It seemed obvious enough to the more scholarly Hindu pupils that he did not know their beloved Sanskrit, the classical Vedic language preserved by the brahmins, though long since extinct in normal public usage. A Sanskrit-speaking pupil named Nana Nimonkar was therefore greatly surprised one day when Sai Baba proceeded to give him a memorable interpretation of a verse from the Sanskrit classic known as the *Bhagavad-Gita*. (45) This explanation had a freshness that was lacking in the orthodox commentaries of pundits, and the sufi made a point of demonstrating a close familiarity with Sanskrit etymology, a revelation to the astounded listener, revealing orthographical significances of which Nimonkar had previously been unaware. Nor were these surprises over, for the exponent told Nimonkar to thereafter read a chapter of the *Gita* before him each day, and he (Sai Baba) would expound the meanings. The teacher kept his word, and this ancient Vedantic manual, itself part of the Sanskrit Epic known as the *Mahabharata*, was thus rendered anew by a nineteenth century sufi adept. This commentary was unfortunately never written down, though the essence of the moment is very rarely adequately preserved in print in those cases where it is worth preserving.

Sai Baba had given proof of superlative accomplishment in an unsuspected area of learning. To assume tht he was illiterate because he did not enthuse about books was a shortcoming of the scholarly mind. He had penetrated the meaning of ancient and not so ancient texts, and he accordingly knew what the immature intellect does with such content.

It was episodes like this that caused the Hindus to gradually appropriate him as a "brahmin." Since many of his pupils were Hindus, he sometimes briefly referred to Hindu scriptures and even the significance of various deities. To him it was irrelevant what people liked to label him. What mattered was the higher development of the human entity, not formulations or ascriptions.

The abovementioned explanation of a *Gita* verse carries strong overtones of Advaita (non-dualism), associated with the tradition of Vedanta that is textually rooted in the Upanishads and the *Gita*. But Sai Baba was an advaitin detached from the commentarial tradition that has tended to narrow down perspectives and cause confusion amongst the pedantic. It has been asserted that he taught the method known as *vichara* or self-enquiry that distinguished the exposition of Ramana Maharshi, (46) and this appears to be accurate, though in other respects these atypical advaitins differed in their methods.

It is still not generally understood that there are important correspondences between Vedantic philosophy and the sufi teaching of *wahdat al-wujud* (Unity of Being). The latter is primarily associated with Ibn al-Arabi, but this can be a historical limitation, (47) since in India particularly, the wujudi philosophy achieved many variants in terms of verbal expression. While many exponents were conceivably only partially fledged in its experiential significations, others like Hazrat Sai Baba appear to have understood that the literary forms are only a focus for the underlying truths that are not nearly so susceptible to ethnic and religious pigeonholes.

At one time, pupils at Shirdi were in the habit of approaching Sai Baba with books that each found inspiring. The objective was to obtain his blessing in their studies. But on one of these occasions a visitor came empty-handed. The others present expected the adept to rebuke this man, but instead Sai Baba gave him an expansive smile and told him that he was wise – since wisdom could not be assimilated by reading even many pages of the *shastras* (scriptures). True wisdom was concealed in one's own *atman* (intrinsic self). Even in respect of understanding meditation, one must first understand the meditator. The human psychology is a mass of contradictions and conflicts, he stressed – how then can a man assimilate anything from the outside? The impressions of such a confused and non-integrated psychology would inevitably be unreliable.

"We have only to see the Self and the rest becomes revealed," he is reported to have said on another occasion. But it is apparent that he considered this to be a rare event. Hence he repeatedly urged some of his pupils, probably the more attentive ones, to: "Think always about this question – 'Who am I?'" (48)

This stress on *vichara* (self-enquiry) did not mean any neglect of the teacher, as is sometimes thought by persons intent upon self-remembering. The essential emphasis in Sai Baba's verbal injunctions was the need for rapport with the teacher. The living potency of his *baraka* was the proof here, something stronger than scriptures or dogmas. Pupils found that stray remarks of his caused an impact out of all proportion to a pedantic analysis of his words. One sentence from Sai Baba was enough to acutely affect someone's life for days, weeks, or even months and years on end. His words might sting or they might heal; none could predict what would come.

His words might be in the form of an instruction, something which had to be carried out no matter what if the pupil wished to continue further. This might well involve the elimination of an undesirable personal trait, or the acquisition of a new and more desirable one – although this would not be explicit in the order given. It might be something which appeared to have no connection at all with the "spiritual life" as normally understood. It is this concrete application to life events which distinguishes the real teacher, something quite apart from standard religio-mystical attitudes.

Despite the acute other-worldliness of much that is reported of Sai Baba, there is evident an atypically "earthy" quality that lends a more striking aspect to his faculties. A Parsi woman left it on record that Sai Baba differed from other saints she had met in not manifesting any state of trance or *samadhi*. "Other saints would forget their body and surroundings and then return to them, but Sai Baba was constantly both in and outside the material world. Others seemed to take pains and make efforts to read the contents of people's minds and tell them their past history, but with Sai Baba no effort was needed." (49)

Mind-reading is not such a particularly advanced faculty as is often thought. Strictly speaking, the above-quoted report is true of lesser men than Sai Baba. The quality of *baqa* characteristics varies considerably. But what is relevant enough is the distinction of such *baqa* characteristics from standard notions of a super-meditative condition entirely divorced from the world of the senses. This latter can provide excuses for the theatrical, varying from trance-mediums to induced paroxysms, none of which relate to *fana*.

Sai Baba does not appear to have been over-partial to people who bothered him for demonstrations of ESP, which has always been a useless distraction in sufi eyes, and indicative of a shallow mentality unsuited to development. Fringe seekers and shallow devotees were often repelled by the Shirdi adept, who sometimes used extravagant shock methods to drive them away. It is quite clear that he wished to be judged by different criteria than those too frequently passing muster under the abused auspices of spirituality.

There is no doubt that Sai Baba was capable of demonstrating bizarre personal characteristics, which gained him the additional appellation of the "mad *faqir*," of appropriate associations with the *majazib* tradition of the Deccan. He did not conform to any stereotyped saintly model; his temperament was very unpredictable, alternating between an amenable placidity and a fiery demonstration of what would normally be construed as anger. He was understandably classified by Meher Baba as a mixture of *jamali* and *jalali* traits – these being attributes of mood in saints and masters according to one of the more evolved sufi formulations. *Jamal* is the disposition of benevolence, amiability; *jalal* is the disposition of "grandeur," authority, reproof, chastisement. Sai Baba could be as gentle as a lamb by all accounts, but when the *jalali* trait predominated, he was capable of venting an explosive rage, even to the extent of dealing blows with a stick to pupils and visitors. But this extreme was comparatively rare; the more usual expression of his displeasure took the form of abusive language, an acute verbal torrent which could stop anybody in their tracks. It was noticed, however, that such volleys were related specifically to individuals; they were nothing of a generalized occurrence. There was a sense of control lent to such outbursts by his habit of suddenly ceasing the tirade and speaking graciously once again, usually to other parties, but sometimes to the chastised. He would then act as if nothing untoward had occurred.

The actual reason for such tirades was not always apparent, though sometimes it was. Visitors of the more inquisitive and acquisitive varieties were frequently the recipients of his disapproval, people whose attitude might in general be summed up as: "I don't really think he is anybody really great, but I had better just take a quick look in case I miss something exciting. I do not approve of his strange ways, but he is becoming rather famous. They say he has occult powers; these I would like to sample, since they may help me to get on in life." When such types approached him, Sai Baba would not only hurl abuse at them, but would also fling stones as if to make doubly sure that he drove them away.

It is said that in nearly all such cases of initially vituperative treatment, the affronted person would eventually discern the teacher's hallmarks of genuine spirituality. In other words, what he was fundamentally attempting to do was to offset pet notions of "spirituality" that amounted to the bogus – in which image he has frequently been caricatured by undiscerning admirers and exploiters.

The effective teacher is not bent upon acquiring a multitude of disciples, much less admirers, devotees, and sentimental acclaim. He may have to make himself seem undesirable at times (even permanently so in some cases) in order to offset the wrong kind of attention.

It would appear that there was method in the madness of the "mad *faqir*." For many years his bed consisted of a simple wooden plank, five feet long by one foot and three inches wide, suspended from the roof of the crumbling mosque by flimsy strips of old cloth. It was not placed near the floor however, but remained suspended about six feet from the ground. A number of his distinctive small lamps were placed precariously upon this plank. Osborne opined that levitation must have been necessary to get on to it and to stay on without breaking the weak supports. (50) Das Ganu, the Hindu pupil to whose book I have made reference, could not resist feeling fascinated by this contraption, and on one occasion carefully took his opportunity to examine it in the company of a few comrades. At this explicit display of curiosity, the sufi erupted into one of his *jalali* outbursts, and smashed the alluring plank into pieces. He was demonstrating the intrinsic worthlessness of this object, which Ganu and the others were making into a fetish by indulging their fantasies of the supernatural. As pupils, he expected something better of them than ill-formed awe of a plank of wood, even if its circumstances were decidedly unusual. In the face of such attachment, the plank had to be relinquished. That is better logic than levitation, a useless feat which has a curious attraction for those who can be easily distracted by meaningless powers.

Sai Baba made it difficult to take him at face value. His manner of speech was highly symbolic on many occasions, though there were instances of reversion to ordinary fact, not least perhaps in order to disturb the routine anticipation of symbolism. He often spoke in parables, not clarifying them, leaving his hearers to assimilate the meanings. Even stray comments or answers to questions were likewise cryptic. Some understood what he was conveying, while others found great difficulty in understanding anything, and some could not follow him at all. There was the well known occasion when a visitor wished to take a photograph of him, and the "mad *faqir*" replied, "No, he is not to take a photograph. It is enough if he knocks the wall down." In his lifetime at least, he was not to become an easy focus for tourism.

Though bizarre in certain features, his lifestyle was uncompromisingly ascetic, save perhaps for his indulgence in tobacco. Even in his more famous years, he still maintained his bearing as the austere *faqir*. He would beg his food daily at five different houses, a fixed number which never changed. At each house he would request in Marathi (since most of the population were Hindu): "Mother, give a little bread." The story has somehow survived that these five houses symbolized the five major world religions.

Returning to the mosque, our *faqir* would place the assorted food he had collected (51) in an earthen pot set aside for the purpose in the compound outside. There he would leave it for some time, and meanwhile anyone and anything was allowed to take what they liked before he himself partook of this fare. The human recipients of this memorable charitability included a poor sweeper woman who belonged to the "untouchable" section of Hindu society, an effective gesture which spoke volumes for his attitude to caste taboos. The non-human recipients included hungry stray dogs, (52) crows, and any others who happened along. He then ate the leavings without any qualms as to hygiene, though he enjoyed robust health.

Sai Baba's day began in a typically allusive manner. After rising, while sitting near his *dhuni* (sacred fire) that burned in the mosque, he would speak to several pupils of distant places he had visited overnight, and of his activities there. He frequently referred to his "travels" over great stretches of space and time, though the information did not reach common ears. Certain of his pupils sometimes slept near him at the mosque, and were well aware that he was physically present at Shirdi the whole night through. But the local schoolmaster was independently convinced that some strange nocturnal activity was in progress. This man lived in a small mud-walled schoolroom immediately behind the mosque, and reported that during the night he could often hear conversations in a multitude of languages, including not only Indian tongues but English also, a matter which he found baffling, since Sai Baba was never known to speak the language of the foreigner on any occasion. As far as is known, the schoolmaster was in full command of his senses. He could not explain the phenomenon, and Sai Baba did not enlighten him.

Inside the mosque, Sai Baba attended to what would normally seem inexplicable rites, for which he never gave any recorded explanation. Das Ganu says that these occurred between one and two o'clock in the afternoon, though only on occasional days. His pupils were not allowed to be present, and he would conceal himself from chance view by a cloth screen. There was nothing exhibitionist in these procedures therefore. Standing before his *dhuni*, he would take out from a purse some ten or fifteen old coins of varying denominations from a quarter *anna* to one *rupee*, and rub them constantly but gently between his fingertips. The surfaces of these coins were eventually worn smooth by this action. He was sometimes overheard to say: "This is Nana's, this is Bapu's, this is Kaka's," and so on with other familiar names of his pupils. But if anyone approached, he would put these coins back in the purse and hide them. One explanation is that the coins acted as "dummies" for the focussing of *baraka* on individual pupils, the most important aspect of guidance on the part of a "guru," or rather *sadguru* to use a less common and less vulgarized term.

Another unorthodox habit of his was to sit behind a pillar in which a lamp resided in a niche and was kept perpetually burning. A Muslim pupil who acted as a personal attendant would fill mud pots with water at his wish and place them near him. Sai Baba would sit with two of the pots beside him and continually pour out water in various directions. Many would deem this a useless pastime on the face of it, though we may be inadequately informed of events, cleaning operations apart.

He spent far more time at the mundane task of bakery. Prominent accoutrements which he kept inside the mosque were a prized set of grinding-stones, and with the aid of these he would diligently make wheat into flour. With the product of this industry he would bake a type of cake, extremely nourishing if simple, in an oven kept outside the mosque. He neither hoarded nor sold the end product, but instead distributed it freely to all and sundry with his accustomed charity.

One hears very little of Sai Baba's relatively down to earth occupations. It seems never to have occurred to his posthumous admirers to emphasize his roles as a country physician and a baker. He can be said to have demonstrated a basic sufi dictum: "The heart with God, the hands for work." But to Narasimhaswami and others, such occupations seemed too ordinary perhaps, even deflating after the more bizarre aspects of Sai Baba's routine. Far better to dwell upon the more weird effects, since these were surely far more important and convincing. In short, the miracle stories were much more in demand.

One day, so the story goes, a group of people saw Sai Baba lying in a field outside the village with his limbs and head lying detached and separate from his body. Whether or not they ran screaming from the spot I have not been able to ascertain, but one imagines that speculation must have been high. I do not propose to relate popular ideas on the matter, and will instead report the more authoritative evaluation from Meher Baba. He appears neither to have substantiated and nor repudiated the factual accuracy of the episode. Surprising though it may seem, he did indicate that such a phenomenon can actually occur, but that it is absolutely irrelevant to higher development. The state was known in sufi lore as *ghousiyat*. According to Dr. Ghani's report, those rare saints who may become subject to *ghousiyat* do not remain under its influence for very long, but quickly outgrow it. Sufis have discouraged speculation over such matters, since weaker psychologies tend to fantasize inordinately at any such opportunity. The fabulation tendency is one of the major obstacles to acquiring knowledge, and is quick to fasten upon any unusual saintly action.

Some readers might imagine that Sai Baba must have exhorted his pupils to become faqirs like himself, to take to the mendicant life and set off to famous places. The truth was very much to the contrary. There are a few cases on record of individuals who wished to follow what they took to be his "example," but he explicitly forbade them to pursue their self-proposed course. Any man who thought that he could imitate Sai Baba might have had to spend the rest of his life in merely getting rid of this idea.

Instead of the ascetic way, the Shirdi adept implemented the mode of life that is emphasized by the sufi dictum: "Be in the world but not of the world" (*Dar dunya bash, az dunya mabash*). In case anyone thinks that this is an easier course, he or she should consider the implications of concentrating upon two things at the same time, rather than upon one only. Any task can be made too easy if it is not attended to properly, notably the path of asceticism, in which exhibitionism can easily replace dedication. Conversely, the person who goes around merely repeating dicta like the one quoted above might just as well proclaim: "This sounds a very convenient way for me to be accounted spiritual while pursuing my materialistic interests; therefore I will gladly shout it from the rooftops."

Not only did this sufi keep his pupils in normal occupations, and in many cases family life, but he also tended to militate against the use of yogic (and dervish) exercises, which have been unintelligently applied for too many centuries. The breathing exercises known as *pranayama* came in for particular discouragement, and he once said: "Whoever proceeds by means of *pranayama* will have to come to me ultimately for further progress." (53) There is indeed evidence of cases in which sadhakas who practiced exercises like those involved in "*kundalini* yoga" found themselves in unpleasant difficulties and had to seek Sai Baba's aid.

The would-be pupil had first to penetrate the layer of eccentricity to find that there was really nothing eccentric about Sai Baba at all. The real eccentricities were in the psychological patterns of the people who saw and heard of him.

"I draw my people to me from long distances in many ways. It is I who seek them out and bring them to me; they do not come of their own accord."

This statement of the Shirdi adept is not open to immediate verification. There are not a few instances recorded of people who were initially drawn to seek him out by his unpremeditated appearance in dreams and "visions" they experienced. This does not necessarily mean that they belonged to the *halka* (inner circle) at the core of the Shirdi situation. The requirements of a disciple are much greater than those of a devotee, though such distinctions are not generally recognized.

According to the reports, there was abundant proof that Sai Baba was aware of the thoughts of those around him. He would often answer unspoken cogitations. In a more dramatic fashion, he would sometimes punish a selfish thought. A simple but graphic illustration of this is reported of the time when he was gifted with pink bananas having a rare flavour. He peeled them and gave them away, as was his habit with such gifts, and one of those present felt an involuntary fear that they would all be consumed before his turn came. Sai Baba immediately peeled another of these exotic fruits, gave it to someone else, and then threw the skin to the concerned party, bidding him to eat that.

One of his distinctive gestures was to touch the head of a pupil; sometimes he would press his hand down heavily upon the cranium, but in other instances merely tap the head or make a movement over it with his fingers. Individual experiences were reviewed amongst his pupils in this connection, and it was concluded that each of these actions caused an instantaneous change in the sensations and feelings of recipients, sometimes very markedly so. This is inevitably open to the charge of imagination from critics. It is said that his physical touch could instantly communicate an experience of expanded consciousness, and one case is on record of a man who lost awareness of his body and surroundings and entered a state of ecstasy. In sufi terms, this can be described as an example of the transference of *baraka*, but it can be duplicated by persons who are not adepts and who merely excite sensations in recipients. It is as well to remember that some people can condition themselves to emotional sensations if they are accustomed to associate these with some authority figure. Fake gurus of spectacular context can easily take advantage of this, and effectively hypnotize the more credulous minds.

The Parsi woman, Mrs. Manager, reported: "One's first impression of Sai Baba was his eyes. There was such power and penetration in his gaze that no one could long look him in the eyes . . ." (54) But a physical description of the man, however compelling, makes for little relevance apart from the inner essentials. It means nothing to the reader that he maintained a short growth of beard, that he had a high forehead, that he wore a plain *kafni* (robe), and that he was often to be seen smoking a *chellum* or clay pipe, a crude article which had to be frequently renewed owing to its short-wearing qualities. One can relate the bare fact that he would sit upon the ground with his pupils, and pass round his rustic pipe amongst them, but again it means nothing in the absence of all the other factors involved in a meeting with Sai Baba. Attention might flicker a fraction more to be told that his exceptionally lustrous eyes could reflect the epitome of gentleness, and yet at any moment were liable to flash with the fiery quality of the *jalali* trait.

The really heavyweight factors concerning him might

well pass unnoticed (as indeed they have) amidst the mass of secondary data, in the sense of designating as primary the intrinsic "function" which he had inherited (in the non-genetic manner) from past human exemplars. This matter of function is not well understood in general, and one is perhaps at risk in attributing to Sai Baba a very high function as has been done elsewhere, (55) since it is apparent that the significances will be lost upon those who are not themselves adepts.

Yet it is perhaps only the concept of "function" that can serve to make clearer the context of the numerous affirmations of gnosis reported of Sai Baba. These seem to have been largely intended as shock statements to make hearers acquaint themselves with aspects of the situation other than the most obvious. In Sufi and Vedantic lore, such affirmations can amount to diluted verbal reflections of an inner state of consciousness. But it is incumbent to remember that any idiot can simply repeat gnostic slogans at third-hand. A certain parrotry commonly afflicts key-phrases of Advaita Vedanta, for instance. Yet Sai Baba's utterances show a distinct originality.

I list here a selection of Sai Baba's translated statements:

"Those who see Baba in Shirdi have not seen him at all."

"I am not this three cubits and a half of the body that is called 'Sai.'"

"My race is that of Parvardigar, (56) my religion is Kabiri, (57) and my profession is to bestow blessings."

"I am formless and everywhere."

"I am God and the universe."

"I am all and in all – in saints, criminals, animals. I pervade the universe. I created Brahma." (58)

"Nothing moves but by my grace." (59)

Two more of these utterances perhaps merit special attention. If it was reported at all accurately, then the affirmation of "I am Allah" (60) would have proved a major stumbling-block to orthodox Muslims. In contrast, "I am Krishna" was much less startling to Hindus, who can usually assimilate such disclosures without so much as batting an eyelid. But a problem exists for those who interpret such statements literally.

It is relevant here to observe that Ramakrishna of Dakshineswar also affirmed his identity as "Krishna." Looking at the matter in a purely literal fashion, Sai Baba and Ramakrishna (d.1886) cannot both have been the celebrated *avatar* of Vishnu. This anomaly is only resolvable in a perspective of inner consciousness and function. "Krishna" represents the supreme realization, the state of real and ultimate being, and more than this even, a special duty to discharge in the world.

Since Sai Baba has posthumously been made into an *avatar* figure, it is worthwhile to point out that definitions of what an *avatar* is are notoriously vague. With regard to his Hindu following, the Shirdi adept identified himself not only with Krishna, but with all the Hindu gods in general. Hence Narasimhaswami reports him as saying: "I am Vithoba. I am Ganapati. All offerings made to Ganapati have reached me. I am Dattatreya. I am Lakshmi Narayan. Why go to seek the Ganga (Ganges) elsewhere? Hold your palm at my feet; here flows the Ganga." This refrain becomes understandable in view of the fact that worship of gods is not remedial by comparison with instruction from a human teacher. The veneration of the Ganges and other traditional features of religion amount to distractions.

Competition with distractions led Sai Baba to emphasize that the exercise of rapport with the human guru was the only viable *sadhana* (discipline). He does not appear to have felt unduly flattered by the attention he received, being realistic in his appraisal of general tendencies of admirers and devotees. "My master told me to give bounteously to all that ask, but nobody asks with wisdom," he observed. "My treasury is open, but nobody brings carts to take away the real treasures. I say 'dig and search,' but nobody wants to take any pains." (61) He was complaining at the way in which visitors approached him for mundane benefits and other secondary considerations. It was inevitable that such people would make too much of "miracles," obscuring facets of a situation which they were unable to perceive.

CHAPTER THREE

THE LAST YEARS

From 1900 onwards, there was a steady growth in the number of visitors to Shirdi, and during the last eight years or so of his life, Sai Baba was inundated with a continual stream of people from distant towns and cities, notably Bombay. This multitude were not all disciples. Some merely looked on in awe, some came along for the ride, many pursued irrelevant desires. Some where critical, full of the new Western ideas which had gained firm ground during the past few decades. Could this *faqir* really be anybody of importance, sitting out of the way in such a shabby rural mosque?

The urban wave included many tradesmen and more affluent businessmen, all alike fired by the new incentives of Western commercial "progress," though they had not forgotten their religious background. They tended to confuse the two sets of values however. Then there were the more intellectually sophisticated, who tended perhaps to demand a place in whatever was going on as their natural right. Many of these products of the new education, in attempting to emulate John Bull and not quite succeeding, had simultaneously lost the dignity supplied by the best in their native traditions. They were at a subsequent disadvantage with Sai Baba, merely substituting a new form of superstition for that of the "uneducated" country people. But the countryman at least possessed an element of humility which was often lacking in his urban superiors. Both forms of superstition, degenerated ancient and ill-adjusted modern, were frequently the victim of craving for the sensational, whether this was imagined in spiritual or miraculous terms. The collective mentality was largely incapable of seeing big things, only of magnifying smaller things that fell within its range.

When a visitor arrived at the Shirdi mosque, if he was not rebuffed, he was likely to be presented with a blunt demand for cash. Sai Baba would specify the exact amount he required, which frequently transpired to be every penny that the visitor carried upon his person. This was particularly galling to the enthusiastic business types. More than this however, as if adding insult to injury, the sufi would proceed to give away all the extorted cash before the very eyes of the stupefied donor. At times he seemed to squander the money, as if to get rid of it as quickly as possible.

During the closing years of his life, a vast amount of money changed hands in this manner. It was said that Sai Baba's income equalled that of a provincial governor, which to the average citizen was a truly fabulous amount. But he never kept any of it, pouring it all away as part of his technique. The government authorities found to their astonishment that they were unable to levy income tax from him – he had no personal fund, no possessions worthy of mention, he begged his food daily, he did not even have an *ashram* (a resident centre where the guru lives with his disciples). On the day he died, there was just enough money available to pay for his funeral expenses.

By the end of each day, Sai Baba had nothing left of whatever cash he had requested from visitors. Narasimhaswami tells us that he gave the cash away to poorer people standing by, that he supported passing ascetics and impecunious devotees, and fed those who otherwise had no means of staying at Shirdi for a while. This redistribution feat did not benefit Sai Baba himself.

He did not solicit everyone in this manner, however. Sometimes when money was freely offered to him, he would refuse to accept it. He once said: "I only ask those whom the Faqir (Allah) points out, and in exchange I have to give them ten times as much."

It was inevitable that some became prejudiced against him in relation to this matter. Some devised various stratagems to elude any substantial payment, but he invariably caught them out. Sometimes he not only took everything a visitor had in his pocket, but asked for more than was available on the spot, so that borrowing became necessary.

Some became aware of a symbolism of numbers where small quantities were involved, realizing that the amount of rupees stipulated represented qualities to be developed or relinquished. Pupils with any experience of the procedure knew that personal attitudes in these situations were of paramount importance. Some were liable to lose not only their aplomb, but also their temper.

Situations that arose in connection with these cash transfers were often amusing to onlookers, though not to those involved.

A rich Hindu arrived by horse and cab from the railway station at Kopargaon. He lost no time in pressing his request for experience of divine reality. "I have come a long way for it," he insisted. "They say that the saint of Shirdi reveals God quickly." He had also heard of the faqir's financial requests, though he kept quiet about this, since he had two hundred and fifty rupees in his pocket. He emphasized Sai Baba's speedy abilities not least because haste in this matter would conveniently offset the losses involved in paying the cab-driver for any extra waiting-time at Shirdi.

The sufi responded with an alacrity that was very gratifying to the petitioner: "Oh yes, don't worry – I will show you God quickly and clearly. This is not a matter that can be delayed. People like you who seek illumination are hard to find. Most people who come here want prosperity or health or freedom from some trouble, or a good position or pleasure or some worldly object. Nobody wants God. How I long to see those who long to see God! One should realize Brahman (Supreme Reality) before death, or there will be an ever recurring cycle of births and deaths. A real guru can give realization and only a real guru can."

This was counsel mixed with tongue in cheek flattery. Immediately afterwards, the sufi said that he urgently needed a loan of five rupees. He then seemed to lose all interest in the seeker of revelation, intent to all appearances upon obtaining the money. A boy was continually sent round to various locals, but each time returned empty-handed. The visitor began to lose patience – each minute was costing him money, though he did not offer the paltry five rupees from his concealed wad of notes. Nor did he despatch the waiting cab, since he was anxious to catch the next train home after acquiring his divine experience. However, he did not neglect to plead to the now preoccupied saint: "Will you help me to know Brahman?"

He was unprepared for the suddenly detailed reply: "That is what I have been doing. Don't you understand? I want five – one must surrender five to attain Brahman. One must surrender the five senses and the five vital forces, and for that one requires detachment. The road to divine knowledge is hard to tread. Not all can tread it. When it dawns, there will be light. Only one who is unattached to things earthly and heavenly alike can attain to divine knowledge."

It becomes obvious why Sai Baba did not cultivate a standard "saintly" image; many conceptions of the "spiritual" are so callow that they cannot be corrected in the time necessary to assimilate truth, unless perhaps some shock impact is successful.

One of Sai Baba's famous sayings is: "I give people what they want in the hope that they will begin to want what I want to give them." The context has so far been largely neglected in the posthumous revelations of the Shirdi revivalists. The recipients of the money which Sai Baba took from visitors were often "those who were not always really worthy." These were individuals who came to Shirdi in the hope of obtaining material benefits. It evidently suited the adept's sense of humour to treat them accordingly in his redistribution feat. Spectators could make of it what they wished, but it would not have been the only site where "fleas" congregated. It is reported that one recipient would receive as much as a hundred rupees daily, and that he used the funds to "live well and sumptuously," though he was also able to support his large family. In contrast, Sai Baba was very ascetically demanding of those who were his disciples. These latter were a minority, and quite distinct from the devotees, visitors, and hangers-on. The young Zoroastrian Gustadji Hansotia also lived at Shirdi, but was never given money, received only scant food, and in general was denied even simple amenities like clothing and blankets. (62) But Gustadji was not detailed in devotee reports like that of Narasimhaswami. It remains to add that "those who were not always really worthy" would not have conceived of their presence in such terms, but instead would doubtless have described themselves as disciples of the Shirdi master. If this was liable to have confused those for whom surface appearances were ultimate yardsticks, the discernment of parasitic elements is nevertheless a useful exercise for those in desperate need of it.

As I have stated earlier, Sai Baba is now mainly remembered by devotees for his "miraculous" achievements. One cannot put the blame entirely upon Narasimhaswami for this lop-sided emphasis, since it was already present amongst the sufi's reputed followers while he was still alive.

In common with other sufis, Sai Baba evidently possessed various healing abilities. Once people grasped that he had these abilities, they flocked to him in the hope of such benefit. They were not content with the odd case of healing, however; they wanted tangible benefits of all kinds, and the above-quoted statement he made to the parsimonious Hindu was no exaggeration it would seem: "Most people who come here want prosperity or health or freedom from some trouble, or a good position or pleasure or some worldly object." One should perhaps add to this list the request for issue to the childless, a common Hindu plea in saintly circles. (63)

Though he was extremely offputting to many visitors for very good reason, he did not always withhold his ability to provide cures for suffering. But while he frequently allowed some latitude in this direction, it was a minor part of an activity which remained unknown to the self-seeking devotee.

His reputation for curative powers developed out of his early ministrations as a herbal doctor. One day he told the attendant who dispensed his remedies not to bother with the various herbs anymore, but from now on to give everyone the same medicine. Sublimate of alum became the unorthodox rule for all comers, and finally he relinquished even the use of this, and would instead merely give a little ash (*udhi*) from his *dhuni* fire. Eager visitors would clamour for this product of incineration, oblivious to whatever else might be available. Narasimhaswami compiled reports of the cures treasured in popular memory. We learn that when responding to a request for healing, Sai Baba would sometimes say "I will do this," but more often he would remark *"Allah achcha karega"* (Allah will put it right) or *"Allah Malik hai"* (Allah is the Ruler).

There were prospective patients to whom he refused to give his aid, no matter how plaintive and desperate the plea. Sometimes he would give a brief explanation, perhaps saying, for instance, that to prolong the life of a sick or diseased person would only result in protracted suffering. But at other times he would not proffer any explanation at all. The petitioners could either feel offended, or else accept that this non-dispensing approach was supported by a knowledge of what could not or should not be done. To his increasing horde of (largely Hindu) supplicants, he would often refer to Allah as "the Faqir," and when refusing a request for healing intervention, he would frequently comment "The Faqir will not let me do that" or "I can only do what the Faqir orders me to."

An unusual instance of Sai Baba relenting after an initial refusal to heal, was the following. One Bhimaji was suffering from a chronic chest disease thought to be tuberculosis. When he was brought to Shirdi, the sufi explained that this disease was the result of past misdeeds, mainly concerning theft, and that he was now a victim of the backlash motion of the normally invisible cause and effect process. The sufi refused to interfere with this process, much to the consternation of Bhimaji's relatives. They begged and cajoled persistently, with all the eloquence they could muster. It was strange to see Sai Baba finally relent and say to the sufferer: "Don't worry. Your troubles are over. The Faqir is all-merciful. He will eradicate your disease. He loves all as his own Self." Bhimaji gradually recovered, but not without experiencing strange dreams in which he suffered intense pain and anguish. (64)

The alleviation of afflicted health, or downright material benefit, were not the only hoped for gains that were pressed. A number of Hindu visitors requested "visions" of their favoured aspect of Deity. He discouraged this almost as much as he frowned upon the desire to achieve powers. One of those who presented himself to the sufi for training had previously undertaken *sadhana* under a former guru and had acquired certain psychic "powers." Sai Baba was forcefully adamant that the candidate had to get rid of these sordid accomplishments before he could be accepted as a pupil, not least because of the damage done in respect of an inflated ego. No real teacher stimulates anyone to a desire for "powers." This obsession is fit only for infantile guru-mania, and can lead to a lifetime's wastage of potentially higher faculties than those vulgarly envisaged. Some find the distractions entertaining and exciting, which says nothing for their capacity to discriminate. The seeker who cannot differentiate in relation to the most basic emphases is better off ignoring all gurus rather than falling prey to a sensationalist who can effectively hypnotize through the victim's own power of self-deception and craving for the magical.

Sufis hold that varying grades of "powers" can be acquired on the inner path. But these are totally incidental to development, and any fixation upon them amounts to a kind of spiritual suicide, since other vital attitudes of mind are thus undermined and corroded.

Many of the so-called "powers" that one hears or reads about today are very elementary psychic extensions, and one does not have to be on the inner path, or even a seeker, to indulge in them. These "powers" are often a ruse by means of which vulgar gurus catch the attention of the uneducated, the objective being to exploit the latter as much as possible.

When Narasimhaswami's book appeared in print, and hundreds of newly enthralled devotees went to make their pact at Shirdi with the departed saint, the popularization maintained a ritual of dispensing the ash from the *dhuni*, which was kept burning at the mosque. The miracle worshippers thought wistfully of how Sai Baba had lit lamps with water, and of how he had placed his hand on the head of a poor man just prior to the latter's achievement of riches. Contrary to popular notions, Meher Baba indicated that one of Sai Baba's real achievements had been a mundane daily occurrence which had never been recognized to have any connection with "powers."

When answering the most basic call of nature, the Shirdi adept would usually spend an hour, and sometimes even several hours in the lavatory for obscure reasons. When his reputation spread abroad, this part of his routine achieved ceremonial overtones. Since the Hindu devotees were by then in the habit of feting him at every opportunity, they would form a procession in his wake at the fixed hour he reserved for his visit to the *lendi*, as he called his primitive toilet, which was situated at some distance from the mosque. This procession became an accepted feature of the village life, and was even accompanied by the local band. The devotional contingent followed him automatically, and he did not stop them, just as he never said why he took so long over the procedure at hand.

The *lendi* procession was largely forgotten after Sai Baba's decease; Osborne, for one, made no specific reference to it. But Meher Baba gave a unique explanation of the event. According to him, sadgurus can control and direct the spiritual, and even the material, welfare of the universe, a contention which reflects the well known belief in sufi lore dating back at least to the time of Hujwiri. But the "masters" usually do this through their agents who are scattered in different parts of the world. These agents hold different jurisdictions in accordance with their level of advancement. Some of these agents who are on "higher planes of consciousness" are "vaguely conscious" of the source of directions that they carry out, but the majority of those on the "lower planes of consciousness" are unaware of the source of the orders which they "implicitly and automatically carry out." This is one reason given for the disparity evident in that many of those who are known and worshipped as saints do not recognize the sadgurus who direct and control affairs of the spiritual hierarchy. "To come to the point," says Ghani's version of Meher Baba's statements, adepts like Sai Baba, "while engaged in the act of evacuating the bowels, at such a time dispense altogether with the agency of saints, and directly control cosmic processes." This explanation seems to be unique. "Believe it or not," adds the same reported source, "it is possible for sadgurus (i.e. qutubs), while thus engaged, to determine and calculate numerically all the forms and stages of evolving creation in detail." (65)

Whether or not this was a tongue in cheek disclosure is best left for the reader to decide. Meher Baba was certainly elevating a mundane physiological occurrence to a greater significance than all the popularly acclaimed "siddhis" events put together.

In some accounts, the place of evacuation is referred to in a different context as the Lendi gardens. Sai Baba is contrastingly described as meditating there for two hours every day, remaining there alone and undisturbed. During those hours, "his aspect was forbidding and stern," to such an extent that "devotees could not go anywhere near him." But soon after his return from the gardens, he would appear relaxed again and his normal self. (66)

It was not by any means usual, though certainly not unique, for a mystical teacher to have a substantial number of both Hindu and Muslim pupils. Sai Baba sometimes spoke of himself as a reincarnation of Kabir, the fifteenth century sufi of North India who was an earlier example of the intercultural tendency at work amongst these two major religious traditions of India. There is no evidence that Sai Baba meant this literally; the immediately relevant context is that his own "religion" was in the Kabir mode, i.e., comprehensive of essential intercultural elements. Whether or not there is truth in reincarnation need not concern us here; even if there is, fake gurus can easily misuse the subject to impress the gullible. Reincarnation has provided other well known loopholes for selfishness; priestly Hindus have for long scrupulously passed by starving men dying at the roadside, saying to themselves reassuringly: "Never mind, he will get another birth. Better luck next time."

The biographical details concerning Kabir are much more sparse than the data on Sai Baba. The former is best known for his poetry, a feature which sets him apart from the Shirdi sufi, though in other respects there are similarities discernible. From Persian sources written in the

Mughal era, it is evident that Kabir was born a Muslim, but ignored the prohibitions of the orthodox *ulama* (doctors of the law) in his affinity with the sufi perspective of *wahdat al-wujud*, a teaching generally associated with Ibn al-Arabi though actually more complex than is commonly detailed. Externalists in the Muslim camp viewed him as having become an infidel (*kafir*), since he considered Hindus his friends. The liberal Muslim prince Dara Shikoh wrote in the seventeenth century that both Hindus and Muslims considered Kabir as belonging to their own religion, though in reality he was far removed from all of them. (67)

It is feasible that Kabir may have expressed something similar to the unorthodox gnostic pronouncements of Sai Baba, who is (with fair reliability) reported to have said: "I am in Gangapur, Pandharpur, and in all (sacred) places. I am in every part of the globe. All the universe is in me."

It should not be imagined that Sai Baba encouraged any doctrinal mergence between Islam and Hinduism. It was no use dwelling upon this, since what he wished to impart does not exist in conventional religion. He did demand a toleration and cooperation between the two factions; he expected his pupils to see beyond the insularities of doctrine.

In situations where quarrels occurred, Sai Baba's favoured method of rebuke was to pose the question: "Who is quarrelling with whom?" This was in reference to his theme of the indwelling self which has been compared with Advaita Vedanta. "Let none hate and let none forget that I, you, and all the world are parts of the Lord," affirmed Sai Baba, (68) though in his case other factors of impact supported the mere verbal insistence.

With the increase in the number of visitors, a stronger Hindu devotional element crept in. In 1908 a child of four went every morning to the mosque and placed a flower on the faqir's head as part of an act of homage. A section of the Hindus were quick to follow this up, and insisted upon performing the *arati* ceremony of worship before him. Sai Baba gave way to their wishes. They would adorn him with flowers, or sandal paste and vermilion, in the spirit of *puja* (worship). But the fact that Hindu worship was being performed in a mosque had a bombshell impact upon Muslims, as he had doubtless anticipated. The more orthodox upholders of Islam were now torn between conflicting loyalties, the teacher or their religious background. Ancient antipathies were forcefully reasserted.

A man who was in constant daily contact with Sai Baba was a certain Rohilla Muslim, of Turko-Afghan background, a descendant of the Rohilla community which had gained a local power at Rohilkhand in North India during the eighteenth century. He tended to outright fanaticism in matters of religion, though so great was his respect for the sufi that he even called him Paigambar, meaning "Messenger of God." Every night he would read the *Quran* before Sai Baba in the mosque. He vehemently protested against the mid-day Hindu worship and its attendant music (a strictly non-religious factor in Islam) which were defiling the mosque in his view. The sufi merely smiled and said, "All that is Allah."

This higher perspective was lost upon the religionist however, even though he might appreciate the sufi breadth in other matters to which his upbringing was less conditioned. He was thoroughly enraged at the detested image worship prevailing in the sacred precincts. It weighed so heavily upon him that he at length decided that if Sai Baba would not put an end to this idolatry, then he would have to put an end to Sai Baba. He had always looked upon the *faqir* of Shirdi as being a staunch Muslim, but felt that Sai Baba was now betraying Islam by such extremist association with the *kafirs* (infidels). How could the sufi allow himself to be worshipped by these polytheists? It seemed an appalling crime, and so one day when the sufi was out walking, the Rohilla came up behind him with a hefty club, burning with homicidal intent. Sai Baba turned around at the crucial moment, touched his attacker's wrist, and gazed into his face. This glance seemed to paralyze the maddened assailant, who sank to the ground as though he himself were the victim. Someone had to help him up, for he was unable to do so himself. When the shock wore off, he decided that it was he himself who had to go, and a few days later he went to bid farewell to Sai Baba. He did so amicably however, and with the sufi's blessing he went his separate way.

Another Muslim pupil was Mir Jaman. He reacted with similar hot-headed fury to the Hindu infiltration at the mosque, but with an important variation, since he did not conclude that Sai Baba should be despatched. One night he sprang up from his place before the sufi in a fit of anti-Hindu reaction. Drawing his sword, he boldly declared that the Hindus were spoiling Sai Baba by worshipping him in their idolatrous manner, and he therewith requested permission to cut their throats. The sufi replied: "It is I who am mad and am responsible for their worshipping me, so if you want to cut any throats, you must begin with mine."

The fiery Mir Jaman calmed down, having to accept that Sai Baba was allowing the Hindus their accustomed expression, even though it be on Islamic territory. It was not easy for such a warrior spirit to bend backwards, but this was what was required.

Sai Baba was now exerting pressure on the Muslims by seeming to favour Hindu customs. The reader should not imagine (as some of the Hindus subsequently did) that he valued Muslims less because of this; on the contrary, it could well mean that he valued them more. He was forcing the Islamic minority to a greater quality of attention through the new situation. The man who has the capacity to turn his back upon conditioned notions deeply ingrained in him from birth, following what then becomes a comparatively invisible directive, has a greater chance of becoming a sufi, other factors being in order. It is easy for the modern Westerner to smile at the shortcomings of traditional culture values, but before smiling, he should pause to consider what the equivalent reversal stress upon twentieth century conditioning would entail. He should also ask himself if he possesses the underlying qualities of character inherent in some of our Muslims – their deep loyalty, their emotional power, their potential to produce Sai Babas.

One palpable effect of the new developments at Shirdi was that Muslim pupils became far outnumbered by Hindus, in view of the orthodox displeasure incurred. It was perhaps Sai Baba's way of cutting down on numbers in one department in order to create a proportionately better standard, even while another department was thrown open to the disposition of a social majority. When newcomer Muslims appeared on the scene, it was harder for them on average to persevere in becoming pupils than it was for Hindus.

Abdulla was a young orphaned Pathan, bred to the highly orthodox sunni tradition of the Afghan domains. He wanted to travel to Mecca, and started out on his own from his home town of Tarbella. He travelled south to Manmad, where he learned that a great sufi lived not far distant at Shirdi, who showered money on such as pilgrims and faqirs, and that this man would surely get him to Mecca. So the young Pathan pilgrim made his way in 1913 to the now famous village.

"As I entered the gate of the mosque, Sai Baba was standing there before me. Our eyes met and I felt at once that he was my teacher." Abdulla remained at Shirdi, finding that Sai Baba fed him along with the small community of faqirs and others who benefited from the constant inflow and expenditure of funds. But though he respected the sufi, he did not understand much about him, and was greatly offended by the constant association with Hindus – whom Abdulla looked upon as enemies. The animosity of this young Sunni Muslim was thinly veiled, and he was aghast at the Hindu worship that was permitted in the mosque. It took three years for him to overcome this bias, and to eventually see the validity of the Hindu point of view. By that time he could see that there was a lot more to staying with Sai Baba than he had at first supposed, and that his attitude upon arrival had been crude. He could see how he had been partly influenced to remain at Shirdi instead of going to Mecca simply because he was well fed and had a roof over his head. Yet he had come to the real Mecca of the day without knowing it.

To all appearances, the rapidly swelling volume of Hindus monopolized Sai Baba from now on, tending to obscure much else that was less obvious. In his *jamali* moods, he allowed his person to be worshipped by the devotional contingent during these last years of his life, and so it was inevitable that the overall impression was created of a Hindu, or Hinduized, guru. At first he showed distinct aversion to the demand for formalism, but since the underlying devotion was of potential value to the multitude now involved, he acquiesced to magnificent annual celebrations in which large crowds watched as he was taken in grand procession, complete with caparisoned elephants, a silver chariot, clouds of incense, and much singing. On these occasions devotees treated him more like a maharaja than a guru, and insisted on bedecking him with jewellery, even though he showed his dislike of this tinsel. The daily *lendi* procession was a smaller and less elaborate version of this communal desire for pageantry.

Yet it was far from being a standard worship situation, even from the Hindu point of view. To start with, there were cases of rigid caste Hindus being disinclined to visit him because he was a Muslim. Once when a brahmin of this frame of mind was reluctantly persuaded to go and see the "Muslim guru," Sai Baba shouted: "Throw that scoundrel out!" Not only this, but the sufi personally chased the visitor away. (69)

Hindu gatherings where devotees come to pay their respects to a holy man are usually decorous affairs marked by due reverence and sanctified behaviour on the part of the respective parties involved. Flabberghasted, wide-eyed Hindus would gaze incredulously upon the equivalent scene at Shirdi, where Sai Baba would carefully amass a pile of stones at his side, and with these frequently pelt various people who approached for his *darshan* (meeting). He was demonstrating that not everybody knew what his *darshan* really entailed, and that some were not ready for it.

Those visitors who were not warded off in some way, and who were not divested of their cash, might still encounter another baffling factor in the form of statements which the sufi made to them. Here is a typical selection: "Your servants' servant I am. I am your debtor. I am purified by your *darshan*. It is grace on your part to have given me the sight of your feet. I am a worm in your excreta."

This verbal reversal of roles had a deeper significance than the surprise element. It provided the key to why he allowed himself to be styled as a "guru," as a recipient of worship, as a man perpetually on call to those who lacked various perspectives. The aspect of service is an accompaniment to an inner function, and entails the highest form of quality vaguely indicated by the abused word love, which is commonly and sentimentally exploited by individuals and groups claiming to be other-worldly. Sai Baba was ruggedly unsentimental in his methods, and for that reason is more convincing.

Hindu devotees were often puzzled as to why the usual guru prescriptions were not forthcoming in his case. He did not, for instance, divide people up between the paths of *bhakti* (love) or *jnana* (knowledge), since in comprehensive development there can be no lop-sided approach. People who concentrate exclusively upon either of these attitudes can lose out on more than they gain.

Would-be pupils of the Shirdi sufi waited in vain for "initiation" of the formal kind so common in India (and amongst dervish movements), and now prevalent in the West also. They had yet to understand that real initiation cannot be reduced to a perfunctory rite that even a simpleton can imitate.

There is one case recorded of a Hindu woman who desperately decided to fast severely until Sai Baba gave her disciplinary instruction, meaning of the kind she was accustomed to thinking of. She imagined that this measure would guarantee a torrent of eloquence upon the subject. After she had gone four days without any food, the sufi sent for her and told her that it was not his way to give the standard forms of instruction (*mantra, japa*, yoga, and so forth), since he followed the example of his guru who was very powerful and whose methods were different and did not involve verbal formulae.

Sai Baba had indeed accepted the Hindu conventions of worship as part of the Shirdi programme to recycle conditioning factors – but he did so upon his own terms, not those of the devotees.

A striking parallel to the general developments of the last years is afforded by the rebuilding of the mosque. Half the roof had caved in, and the rest of it seemed likely to follow. The Hindu majority wanted to build a separate place of residence for him, but he could not be induced to leave his mud domicile, crumbling though it was. They asked his permission to rebuild the mosque, deeming it a demolition job, but he refused. They kept pressing their request to no avail, until one of the devotees (a Revenue inspector) dumped cartloads of stone in front of the building, announcing that he was going to begin the work of renovation. The sufi told him to take the stones away and use them to repair the local Hindu temples. This was not done however, and finally Sai Baba allowed the proposed rebuilding to begin. Yet he constantly interfered and frequently destroyed what had been achieved, much to the puzzlement of the labourers. At this time he was staying alternate nights in the mosque and guest-house (*chavadi*), another simple mud erection. The devotees could only work without interruption during those nights when he frequented the latter place. Even while disturbing the building venture, he gave instructions concerning its procedure, a contradiction enough to offput any labourer but which a pupil was expected to bear with.

To these harassed Hindus, he fastidiously insisted upon regulation Islamic architecture, complete with minarets and a *nimbar* or recess in the sacred west wall (facing Mecca). Yet in contrast to the Islamic features, he incorporated a special fireplace, and this *dhuni* was kept perpetually fuelled and alight in accord with his established practice. Another innovation was a seat made for his special use, with a low balustrade to lean upon, adjoining the *dhuni*. When the building was at long last finished, he referred to it as a "brahmin mosque," not necessarily any reference to a Hinduization, since he is reported to have used the word brahmin (the English corruption of *brahman*) in the sense of a spiritual orientation. This new mosque was built by Hindus, and largely attended by Hindus, but it remained an Islamic feature of the landscape (though it seems no longer to have been used for the public worship of Muslims). The Hindus referred to it as Dwarka Mayi ("mother of mercy"), and believed that karmic sufferings ended when one climbed its steps. It seems ironic that Sai Baba's frequent assertion of "The Guru is all the gods" occurred in a mosque, but there is more than one form of iconoclasm.

Some readers will possibly be thinking that it was a great pity that Sai Baba should have allowed the devotional form of expression to manifest itself at all. In this connection, two factors should be taken into account:

(a) Sufis have been known to step up the rate of external communications at the end of a life span, allowing for greater numbers to be drawn into their work, on the inevitable principle of a little each for many. This final burst of activity, which frequently drains them of special reserves, can be compared, however inadequately, to the culminating sprint of a long-distance run. The athlete knows he is going to finish, and so puts all his energy into this last acceleration, even though it might wind him. There is no comparison (save in confused minds) with the publicizing efforts of copyists. Testimony of numbers alone is useless, since mere indoctrinators have succeeded in mass conversion, with a lack of inner effectiveness comparable to that of repeating slogans from television commercials.

(b) Sincere devotion, though it might appear incongruous to more mental types, can sometimes prove a trigger for a special emotional force required to commence a higher line of development. It also often ensures a certain amount of humility, a vital attitude. This does not of course apply to the more shallow forms of devotion.

A devotee at Shirdi, gazing round at the crowd assembled in Sai Baba's proximity, began to wonder if all of these people were really receptive. Could they all really be deriving deep spiritual benefit? He could clearly see that there were many different types and attitudes represented amongst the throng; were the effects of *darshan* the same for all of them? He voiced his query to the sufi, who replied by pointing to a nearby mango tree that was in blossom, commenting: "What a splendid crop it would be if all the blossoms turned into fruit, but do they? Most of them fall off. Very few remain."

One man who appears to have gone much further than many others was Professor G.G. Narke, who taught geology at the Deccan Gymkhana College of Engineering. This product of Western academic training transpired to be a perceptive pupil of Sai Baba. He proved that an intellectual background need not be at loggerheads with matters customarily deemed to be exclusively "intuitive." Profound "intuitives" are often the most unperceptive individuals, being disguised egotists of the worst kind. By comparison, some "intellectuals" achieve humility more easily.

However brilliant he was in his own field of study, Narke knew from the start that he could not apply his knowledge of mineral formations to Sai Baba. On the contrary, he accepted that he was a child in Sai Baba's department of knowledge, and accordingly exercised a due humility. Here are some of his words concerning his teacher:

"Anyone who judged him from the outside was very far out in his appraisal. Baba was adapting himself to the capacity for understanding of the people who came to him for help. Most of them were superficial and sought only material benefits, and to them he did not reveal his inner nature. But when anyone capable of diving deeper came to him, he revealed more of himself and his true powers . . . He had the peculiar art of giving information to particular individuals in the midst of a group in a way that they alone could understand and not the other members of the group. Strangely enough, at one and the same time he could and did benefit many people by a few words or acts . . . To one deeply observing him the startling fact came out into greater and greater prominence that Baba was living and operating in other worlds besides this world, and in an invisible body. Remarks made by him openly would be treated as meaningless ranting by those who did not know him . . . Sai Baba never spoke untruth, never spoke meaningless jargon, but only those who were familiar with his ways could make out the meaning of what he said or did – that is, when it was intended for their understanding." (70)

The Shirdi sufi may be said to have taught Narke (though not bombastically or rhetorically) how to make a more advanced use of his intellectual powers: how to focus them at the right time and to switch them off when other qualities were needed. The correct proportion of both mental and emotional energy is needed for inner development. The majority of seekers tend to have one or the other predominant, though without necessarily being obvious "intellectuals" or "emotives." The intellect-based psychology constantly misses the cue for a different response pattern conducive to experiential quality, while the more emotive tend to be swamped by irrelevant feelings at the wrong times. It is very difficult making references to higher emotion or higher knowledge, because the unadjusted mind confuses both of these with their inferior counterparts.

Professor Narke acquired the initial discrimination to detect red herrings which customarily bedevil analysis of "spiritual teachers." He commented, "The guru does not teach, he radiates influence." The expository aspect of some purported gurus is indeed sufficient to send anyone to sleep, but the difficulties of assessing a less obtrusive training should not be underestimated. Narke quotes Sai Baba's words: "Stay with me and keep quiet; I will do the rest." In the absence of Sai Baba's shock qualities, any imitator can make such statements and seal a fate of intellectual suicide in the gullible.

Bhakti elements wore off on Professor Narke which, in his case, might be considered proof of progress. But many others who went to Shirdi were automatic in their sense of submission to a higher will, and tended to over-simplify the attendant requirements as a result. It was instinctive on their part, and not to be confused with bringing under control the restless intellect. It is too seldom taken into account by "aspirants" that a person lacking in intellectual capacities has not the advantages of a strong intellect once this is brought under control.

In the available literature on Sai Baba, one will not find reference to his most important disciples, an omission in keeping with other aberrations of reporting, and a striking example of how the highest sufi training so often conceals itself. Incredibly enough, writers like Osborne made no mention of the subject's direct successor (who was by birth a Hindu). This omission will be rectified in Part Two of this book, but it is not necessary to go quite so high as this in order to find other substantial losses of the Shirdi revivalists.

Gustadji N. Hansotia was a Parsi by birth, a member of

the Zoroastrian community in India which had been in process of emigration from Iran over many centuries. He was born in 1892 at Hansota in Gujerat (Western India), and at about the age of seven was sent to Bombay for his schooling, living with his aunt. Intelligent and sensitive, as he grew up he developed a pronouncedly mystical train of thought, and was in reaction to both the orthodox religious outlook and the tendency to Western materialism which were characteristic of the Parsi community. Alongside his secular learning he pursued a study of sufi and other mystical literature that was available to him, with special emphasis upon the biographies of saints and masters. During his teens he maintained a lifestyle of strict discipline, and was particularly noted for his kindness to animals in the spirit of *ahimsa* (non-violence). Possessing a contemplative attitude of mind, he showed little interest in material pursuits when the time came, though he did take a job and regularly gave his earnings to his family – meaning his relatives, since he would not marry. He wished to find a teacher who could competently direct his inner search for truth; he did not want to tie himself to extra responsibilities before he fully understood the spiritual ABC of life, let alone the XYZ factors.

Busy, teeming Bombay held no attractions for Gustadji, though his fellow Parsis were usually enthusiastic enough over its commercial prospects. He felt like a fish out of water, but where was he to go that held the answer to life? He was not to know yet that the metropolis harboured several sufi saints, and that one of the most distinctive sufis of the age, namely Hazrat Babajan, had graced its bustling, grimy environs at the time he had arrived there as a young schoolboy. Later he was to meet Babajan at Poona, but it was not her whom he principally trained under.

When he was about eighteen years old, he came to hear of Sai Baba, and made the journey to Shirdi. This was about 1910, at the time when the major onrush of new devotees was beginning. But Gustadji was more than a devotee. His first visit resulted in several more, and like others who experience something deeper than average, he was later reticent concerning these occasions. What we do know is that he was very soon living as a personal attendant of the Shirdi sufi, having won his way to the centre of the activity at the rural mosque.

His training was not to be easy. As a pupil of unusual potential, he could bear greater pressure accordingly. Gustadji came directly into line with the development schedule at Shirdi, fully operative in what is sometimes known as the "inner circle." The pace in this department is much faster and more demanding than for the majority; there is no question of exclusivism, since those who have not developed the special stamina for it cannot meet its requirements, though some form of exposure to the relevant influences may occur. That at least is the gist of the extrapolations that can be made from the relevant sufi lore.

Many of the curious who read about such things as "inner circles" immediately imagine that great privileges and honours must be entailed, not to speak of advancement or powers. Many glory-seekers entertain thoughts of the "elect" simply because of the distinction they think it will give them if they attained rank (though many automatically assume such rank). Gustadji might have advised such people in his day that they should seek fame in places other than Shirdi, since a knowledge of what is actually involved in matters of rank is contrary to leisurely desires for spiritual status.

Sai Baba did not bestow upon Gustadji Hansotia any special favours as normally interpreted. Instead he put him through a gruelling novitiate, designed to evoke greater efforts in him than others were able to accomplish. The pattern involved both physical hardship and psychological stress. He was to a certain extent prepared for the former by his past self-discipline, but the latter was something unknown.

In later years Gustadji never spoke much of these times, particularly in view of the fact that words became superfluous to him. In course of time this training was continued, though in different forms, under two other teachers. The reminiscences which did filter through lend to the closing years of Sai Baba a far deeper relief than the popular version.

The devotee gloss completely leaves out the marrow of Sai Baba's work with inflated egos, one of the most difficult subjects to explain or understand. There were some whom he caused to feel privileged who merely desired attention, while using these instances in specific situations to test others who were not (or should not have been) pursuing such ends.

There was a complex, many-sided interplay in the matter of the money which Sai Baba constantly demanded and scattered to the winds, only partly captured in the popular version. While it is true that he frequently gave the money away to poor villagers, he often distributed cash to individuals of more parasitic characteristics. As stated earlier, many came to see him in the hope of gaining material benefit, and he did not always disappoint them. Hangers-on appropriated the cash, but one of those who lived on the bread-line was Gustadji. He attended upon Sai Baba day and night, was unstinting in his services, and did not hesitate to carry out the instructions he was given, however difficult these were. Yet the sufi appeared to treat him with scant consideration, and continually withheld from him even the bare necessities of life. There were times when he had to go without food, though others fed to surfeiting, and items such as new clothing and blankets for the colder nights were simply non-existent for him. Surface observers, and pupils of small degree, were likely to think that he was failing in some way, that he was nobody of real consequence. They could not know what his inner contact with the adept involved, any more than they knew the requirements of a disciple, which involve the severe pruning of egoistic manifestations at some critical juncture. In sufi situations, the will has to be broken, and remoulded to a new strength impossible for ordinary psychologies.

Disciples fit a different category to the majority of pupils and devotees. It was because he belonged to this rarer category that Gustadji survived the Shirdi situation in a way that many others did not. While they stood still, he kept pace with new developments. Shortly before the end, Sai Baba directed him to train under another teacher, his own chief disciple who had been prepared to become his successor. This redirection happened to very few at Shirdi, since most were not sufficiently prepared to make the graduation to the new adept's methods. (71)

Another activity of Sai Baba's that largely reaped oblivion was his long-established contacts with the world of migrant ascetics – faqirs, qalandars, sadhus, yogis, and others. He was apt to be extremely hospitable even to the most shallow of these, and some stayed near him for varying periods.

Devotees never seem to have associated this aspect of his work with various of the saints who established themselves in this part of the Deccan during the forty years or so of Sai Baba's residence at Shirdi. Some are known to have expressed great respect for him, though apparently never meeting him. One such was Brahmachari Bua, a Hindu saint only a few miles away at Kopargaon, site of the nearest railway station.

As with Banemiyan Baba, the *majzub* of Aurangabad, the inner links were lost to general view. Devotees usually become obsessed with pedestalling their own teacher exclusively, unable to appreciate the connections elsewhere. Most of Sai Baba's general following never grasped that his successor was living just around the corner at one period, and after Sai Baba's death they ignored this successor – who was even then based just a few miles down the road from Shirdi.

At the time of the First World War, Sai Baba was an old man, frail by comparison with earlier years. His health gradually weakened, and he suffered severe asthma. Yet still the old fiery demeanour persisted on occasions.

In appearance he seems to have remained much the same. His attire was a nondescript robe that might have been worn by either a Muslim or a Hindu. His hair was short, and concealed beneath a piece of cloth tied around his head. There was nothing ostentatious in this garb.

Only in his old age did he relax his severe discipline of begging for his food, and would instead partake of food offered by visitors. But in other ways he would not compromise his ascetic habits. He did not possess any spare clothing, and it was useless to gift him with clothing, since he would immediately give it away. His *kafni* (robe) remained on his body until it was torn with wear; it is reported that some devotee would have to forcibly remove it and make him put on a fresh garment. Yet he was also known to stubbornly repair the old robe, patching it with a needle and thread in accordance with dervish ideals. Yet interestingly enough, mortification as an end in itself was frowned upon by Sai Baba, who was known to say that penitential fasts were useless endeavours. Purity in mind and heart had priority with him; his emphasis was that austerities can be dangerous (to the ego) if they do not serve an inward purification. Even dietary habits came under his displeasure if they were merely habitual protocol; he sometimes made orthodox Hindus eat onions against their will, and did not insist upon the favoured abstinence from meat. (72)

During the Great War, he would regularly visit the main Hindu temple in the village. He would only allow the *arati* worship to occur at a spot mid-way between the mosque and the temple. While this Hindu ceremony was being performed before him, his face is reported to have been suffused with a radiance that was noticeable to all who witnessed it. This may of course represent an exaggeration of the miracle mentality, which effectively opted for the second of the alternatives specified in the following gnostic statement of the adept: "Meditate on me as pure bliss (*anand*), but if you cannot do this, then meditate on this 'Sai' body as you see it with your physical eyes."

Halfway through the war, on 15th October 1916, he exhibited what resembled a sudden attack of frenzy, crying out that it was his day of "crossing the frontiers." Uncharacteristically, he tore off his clothes and moved about stark naked for two hours until this powerful mood subsided. This bizarre behaviour was subsequently thought to have been a foreshadowing of his death, since he died two years later on exactly the same date.

When the end came, there were few who were prepared for it, though he gave various advance warnings. He sent some devotees back to Bombay who had intended to stay, and detained others who were due to leave. He said farewell to a pupil who visited him every fortnight, telling him to discontinue his visits. To another sufi (73) he sent the following message: "The light that Allah lit He is taking away." It is said that the recipient shed tears in response.

It was the time of the Hindu feast of Dasara, and he gave two hundred rupees to buy food for faqirs, who sat chanting prayers and reading the *Quran*. Sai Baba had been ill for a few days prviously, and when morning dawned on October 15th 1918, he was still sick. The day's events were to come as a shock to all those living at Shirdi.

During all his years at the mosque, Sai Baba had kept with him a brick to which he attached a peculiar significance, even using it as a pillow. He said that it had been given to him by his master (assumed in the literature to have been "Venkusa"). On this particular day however, this brick was accidentally dropped on the floor, shattering into fragments. Sai Baba glanced at the pieces and said inscrutably: "It is not the brick that is broken, but my *karma*. I shall not survive its breaking." (74)

About mid-day he sat up, and after a short while sent out those who were with him to take their lunch. Only two brahmins remained with him inside the mosque. He gave one of them some private instructions and then suddenly said: "I am going. Carry me to the *wada*. Only brahmins will be near me." These were his last words. Nana Nimonkar hastily poured water into his mouth, only to find that it spattered out again. Sai Baba expired while leaning against one of the brahmins.

The *wada* he had referred to was a large stone building erected at Shirdi some years previously by a Hindu devotee. In the wake of the initial shock at his sudden decease, there was a controversy over his burial, since the Muslim contingent maintained that he was one of them, and should therefore be buried by them in a separate building that they would specially construct. The civic authorities resolved the issue by drawing up two petitions for signatures, a somewhat loaded recourse in that there were far more Hindus involved than Muslims. (75) The upshot was that Sai Baba's remains were interred in the *wada*, though the corpse was not cremated in the usual Hindu fashion. The divided claims over his funeral rites have aptly been compared with the instance of Kabir, the details of which are more legendary. (76)

One of those who carried the bier of the deceased sufi to the *wada* was Gustadji Hansotia. He was one of the very few who knew the extensions into the present of a teaching situation that had just finished and become part of the past. The majority were unreceptive to fresh developments, and in the absence of a public broadcast from Sai Baba, they assumed that he had not appointed any successor.

Relic hunters scoured the mosque and its compound for the remains of the hundreds of disused clay pipes which had accumulated over the years. The usual railings were erected at strategic points, since the mosque and tomb were now preserved as pilgrimage sites. More than this however, the *dhuni* was kept burning, and devotees elected to give out the ash (*udhi*) to those who desired it as of old. Healings are reported to have continued, and the invisible influence of the guru was said to be still at work even as he had predicted.

It is on record of how one of the Shirdi devotees visited Narayan Maharaj of Kedgaon in 1927. A decade after Sai Baba's death he felt the need for a human representative, but was still very much attached to past memories and associations. The sadguru of Kedgaon told him: "Yours is a supreme guru. He is of a higher rank than I. Why have you come here? Your choice of a guru is excellent. Go to him and you will achieve your purpose." This episode has been treated as a testimony to superfluous association with living teachers. But even if it was accurately reported, there are certain complexities which should not pass unheeded. Narayan Maharaj was a saintly Hindu who was habitually self-effacing, and he was under no obligation to take on pupils who were unsteady on their feet outside a familiar situation. He had also personally known Upasni Maharaj, a disciple of Sai Baba whom to Narayan and others was effectively identical to the Shirdi adept by virtue of successorship. But not everyone could see this, and public advertisements were not in vogue amongst these particular gurus of unusual calibre.

Hazrat Sai Baba of Shirdi is certainly not to be confused with those gurus who announce themselves as speedily returning reincarnations of him, and who even appropriate his name. (77) It should not surprise anyone to learn that such latter day gurus totally emphasize his importance in the miracle department, though in a manner which puts Narasimhaswami in the shade, since at least this inadequate source of information did not seek to substantiate and publicize his own miracle performances.

Like his contemporaries Hazrat Babajan and Hazrat Tajuddin Baba, the Shirdi sufi left no doctrine or sect for posterity to fasten upon and abort for non-relevant purposes. It was left to Narasimhaswami to dig up the miracle stories, but at least this is a readily transparent fixation which will not mislead serious seekers. It was less harmful in some ways than a half-truth doctrine with the kernel omitted, of the type that so often effectively blunts potentiality in those too easily contented.

NOTES

(1) Mani Sahukar, *Sai Baba, the Saint of Shirdi* (first edn, 1951; third edn, Bombay: Somaiya, 1983), pp. 21–3, and citing Hemadpant, *Sai Charita*, and also deeming a statement of Shri Aurobindo to give validity to the theory of Sai Baba's "immaculate origin." Sahukar's account in general draws heavily upon the books of Swami Narasimhaswami, for whom see below, note 6.

(2) For one of the more uncritical observations on this subject, see *ibid.*, pp. 89 ff. However, there is nevertheless an element of reserve discernible. The writer refers to the namesake's "bizarre miracles of producing 'udhi' (sacred ash) from empty space and the materialization of all kinds of silver and gold images and rings from his mouth." This is further observed to "give one a queer feeling of apparent showmanship which is not attractive" (p. 90). Tricks of sleight of hand and related devices are well known in India as a resource for some sadhu types. Like snake-charming, these effects are very extroverted, and vastly inflated by gossip. Cf. Howard Murphet, *Sai Baba: Man of Miracles* (London: Frederick Muller, 1971), for an account of Satya Sai Baba of Puttaparti.

(3) See Shepherd, *Vivekananda: his life and teaching* (forthcoming).

(4) A very passable biography is that of Arthur Osborne, *Ramana Maharshi and the Path of Self-Knowledge* (new edn, London: Rider, 1970).

(5) A. Osborne, *The Incredible Sai Baba* (Calcutta 1957; London: Rider, 1958; rev. edn, 1972). Citations are from the first edition, which was basically unaltered.

(6) Narasimhaswami was President of the organization known as the All India Sai Samaj, based at Madras. This Samaj published his books. He died in the 1950's. Osborne met him before his death, and made an uncritical use of his books, though in a much improved format.

(7) Kishan Singh, "At Sakori With Baba," *The Glow* (Dehra Dun, 1975) 10 (2): 4, 20, reporting statements made in September 1954.

(8) See Shepherd, *Meher Baba, an Iranian Liberal*, part 4 (forthcoming).

(9) Sahukar, cited, p. vii.
(10) E.g., Rao Saheb H.B. Mehta, *The Spiritual Symphony of Shree Sainath* (Bombay, 1952). Sainath was one of the names accruing to Sai Baba. Mehta was a lawyer who refers to other members of the legal profession who visited the saint. Despite the element of first-hand reporting, the interpretation is in the devotional mould, as the title indicates.
(11) Osborne, *The Incredible Sai Baba*, pp. 15–16.
(12) C.B. Purdom, *The Perfect Master* (London: Williams & Norgate, 1937), p. 26. Purdom's entry is only a single page, but nonetheless relevant. He had also heard of the "miracle" story of lighting a lamp filled with water, "which I repeat as told me." Purdom had not been to India at that date, and was given information by persons connected with Meher Baba's ashram.
(13) A summary of Das Ganu was given by Abdul Ghani Munsiff in his article "Hazrat Sai Baba" in *The Meher Baba Journal*, Vol. 1 (Ahmednager, 1938–9). Dr. Ghani was a pupil of Meher Baba, and an Indian Muslim who had a strong interest in Sufism, a subject in which he had an above average erudition.
(14) Sahukar, cited, p. 25.
(15) On this subject, see, e.g., J. Spencer Trimingham, *The Sufi Orders in Islam* (Oxford: Clarendon Press, 1971).
(16) Osborne was less precise in reporting the birthplace as "a small town in Hyderabad State" (*op. cit.*, p. 16).
(17) Osborne, p. 19.
(18) There are discrepancies in other accounts. For instance, the village of Patri has been named as his probable birthplace, and Selu becomes substituted for Shelwadi. See, e.g., Murphet, cited, pp. 19 ff.
(19) Cf. Osborne, p. 19, whose report names the place of occurrence as Selu. Sai Baba said he had stayed with Venkusa for twelve years, which Osborne was inclined to interpret as symbolical, though this number would fit Das Ganu's account.
(20) For a biography, see Shepherd, *A Sufi Matriarch: Hazrat Babajan* (Cambridge: Anthropographia Publications, 1986).
(21) A.G. Munsiff, *art. cit.*, dated Sai Baba's birth at 1856 on the basis of Das Ganu's account. Osborne followed Narasim-

haswami, and did not bother to stipulate even an approximate date of birth, so vague was his basis for chronology. My own inclination would be to render Sai Baba's date of birth as *circa* 1850.

(22) Ramjoo Abdulla, "Meher Baba's Fiery Life and External Activities (Pt 3)," *The Awakener* (New York, 1953) 1(2): 22–5, p. 23.

(23) For more accurate versions of Meher Baba's statements, see Bal Natu, *Glimpses of the God-Man Meher Baba Vol. 3* (Myrtle Beach, South Carolina: Sheriar Press, 1982), p. 236; Eruch B. Jessawala, *The Ancient One*, ed. by N. Anzar (Englishtown, New Jersey: Beloved Books, 1985), p. 24, who states that Zarzarizarbaksha lived seven hundred years ago.

(24) S.A.A. Rizvi, *A History of Sufism in India Vol. 1* (New Delhi: Munshiram Manoharlal, 1978), p. 253, citing an epistle in *Maktubat-i Gisu Daraz.*

(25) *Ibid.*, p. 251.

(26) S.A.A. Rizvi, "The Muslim Ruling Dynasties" (245–265) in A.L. Basham, ed., *A Cultural History of India* (Oxford: Clarendon Press, 1975), p. 254.

(27) John A. Subhan, *Sufism: Its Saints and Shrines* (1938; repr. New York: Samuel Weiser, 1970), p. 235. This early attempt to chart the history of Indian Sufism contains many inadequate perspectives.

(28) For a biographical treatment of Hallaj, see chapter eight of my *Sufis, Batinis, Scientists and Philosophers of the early Islamic era.*

(29) On this and related episodes, see Shepherd, *Minds and Sociocultures*, Appendix 1, nn. 43–46.

(30) For a reflection on nomenclature, see Shepherd, *Psychology in Science* (Cambridge: Anthropographia Publications, 1983), pp. 54–5.

(31) R.M. Eaton, *Sufis of Bijapur 1300–1700* (Princeton, New Jersey: Princeton University Press, 1978), pp. 62 ff. For a contemporary Shia ruler of Hyderabad, see H.K. Sherwani, *History of the Qutb Shahi Dynasty* (New Delhi: Munshiram Manoharlal, 1974), pp. 397 ff. Sultan Muhammad Qutub Shah (rgd. 1611–26) is here described as a highly moral Shi'i who was well versed in both the traditional and rational sciences, and who allowed the fullest latitude for discussion

"without reserve" at learned gatherings. The influx of Iranian emigrants into the Deccan was perhaps never greater than during this period. There was a rapid accumulation of manuscripts in the royal library at Hyderabad, and a "large number of useful books" were compiled during this reign, including books on medicine. *Tasawwuf* (sufism) appears to have been a favoured subject amongst the bibliophiles, and the Sultan himself wrote mystical poetry that contrasts well with the verses of his predecessor. However, literary penchants do not prove wise rulership. During the next two reigns at Hyderabad, there was a revival of the linkage between the Hindu and Muslim cultures, a linkage that had been suspended by the Iranization of the kingdom (*ibid.*, p. 412).

(32) Eaton, cited, pp. 283 ff., 192–5. For an account of the Pratapgarh confrontation, see J. Sarkar, *Shivaji and his Times* (third edn, London: Longmans Green & Co., 1929), pp. 59 ff.

(33) Eaton, pp. 203–4.

(34) Cf. Eaton, pp. 243 ff, who tends to generalize in some respects. One can well agree with Eaton that the *majzub* phenomenon is not to be deplored as proof of the "decay" of Sufism as specified by A.J. Arberry and other scholars (*ibid.*, p. 281). Conventional Sufism had been in decay for a lengthy period, but misnomers should be recognized for what they are.

(35) On Sarmad and Dara Shikoh, see my *From Oppression to Freedom*, Part Two.

(36) For a biography of Tajuddin Baba, see the final chapter of my *Survey of the Sufi Phenomenon* (forthcoming).

(37) S.A.A. Rizvi, "Islam in Medieval India" (281–93) in Basham, ed., *A Cultural Hist. of India*, cited, pp. 292–3. The Chishti disciple was Shah Nizamuddin (d. 1730), who settled in Aurangabad.

(38) On the Kaivanis, see Shepherd, *From Oppression to Freedom*; *id.*, *The Resurrection of Philosophy*, chapters eight and nine.

(39) Trimingham, *The Sufi Orders in Islam*, p. 306.

(40) Percival Spear, *A History of India Vol. 2* (Harmondsworth: Penguin, 1970), pp. 240–1.

(41) Osborne, *The Incredible Sai Baba*, p. 13.

(42) Sahukar, cited, p. 23.

(43) I follow Dr. Ghani, *art. cit.*, in extrapolating this detail, though very little is known of Sai Baba's practice in this respect during these erratically recorded years.

(44) E.g., D.E. Stevens, ed., *Listen Humanity* (New York: Dodd, Mead & Co., 1957), p. 248. Meher Baba had himself met Banemiyan at Aurangabad at the time of the First World War.

(45) For a full report, see Osborne, pp. 22–28.

(46) Sahukar, cited, pp. 25–6.

(47) Some scholars have identified Arabi's teaching as "theistic," and hence deem it nearer to the Vishishtadvaita of Ramanuja than to Advaita proper. This does not take account of the respective audiences involved.

(48) Sahukar, cited, p. 57.

(49) The identity of this informant survives in Narasimhaswami's record as Mrs. Manager; she came from a distant town and probably met Sai Baba in his later years. Cf. Osborne, pp. 32–3.

(50) Osborne, p. 32.

(51) Some Hindus came to assume that he was a vegetarian like themselves in matters of diet, since he ate vegetarian food. It is perhaps more accurate to observe that he ate whatever he was given, which happened to be vegetarian food from Hindu homes. He is reported to have occasionally cooked meat and distributed it to all and sundry (Sahukar, p. 53).

(52) It seems that if ever there was any meat from Muslim homes, it went to these mangy strays, whose plight was often a grim one.

(53) Osborne, p. 106, and remarking on the similarities with Ramana Maharshi.

(54) *Ibid.*, p. 39.

(55) It was Meher Baba who awarded Sai Baba a specific status using sufi terminology, though no commercial publicity was employed. This status is that of the *qutub-e-irshad*, head of the "invisible hierarchy" of saints. A statement to this effect did not appear in print until 1961, and even then was indirectly included in an explanation on compassion which Meher Baba gave at the specific request of his pupil Irene Conyboare, the daughter of the Oxford scholar Dr. F.C.

Conybeare. See Irene Conybeare, *In Quest of Truth* (Kakinada, Andhra Pradesh: Swami Satya Prakash Udaseen, 1961), p. 304. The brief reference to Sai Baba has to date largely escaped attention.

(56) A word of sufi associations signifying God as Sustainer, and which Sai Baba used to designate a category of adepts.

(57) Of Kabir, i.e. following the example of Kabir, the fifteenth century sufi who taught both Muslims and Hindus. On this, see chapter three.

(58) God the Creator, first aspect of the Hindu trinity.

(59) These statements were included in A.G. Munsiff, *art. cit.*

(60) This was included by C.B. Purdom in *The God-Man* (London: George Allen & Unwin, 1964), p. 23. It is my own inference that Sai Baba's original wording had the sense of the Arabic term *hujjat-Allah*, the "Proof of Allah," a phrase used in classical Sufism.

(61) This comes from Narasimhaswami's *Sri Sai Baba's Charters and Sayings*, which gives some interesting material not always well integrated in the biographical sketches.

(62) Irene Conybeare, cited, pp. 304–5.

(63) It is certainly not exclusive to Hindus however. An English woman, the wife of the District Revenue Commissioner, once requested this boon of Sai Baba. See Osborne, pp. 55–6.

(64) This episode appeared in A.G. Munsiff, *art. cit.*, who gives the explanation that the "karmic debt" had to be expiated by the pain suffered in the dream state.

(65) *Ibid.* The date of this explanation is not recorded by Dr. Ghani.

(66) Sahukar, pp. 36, 54–5, making no reference to the toilet.

(67) S.A.A. Rizvi, *A History of Sufism in India Vol. 2* (New Delhi: Munshiram Manoharlal, 1983), pp. 411 ff. For a more detailed discussion of Kabir, see my *Survey of the Sufi Phenomenon*.

(68) Sahukar, p. 58.

(69) This man later gained a deeper connection with Sai Baba. For fuller details, see Osborne, pp. 76–7.

(70) This is one of the more discerning testimonies in the varied pages of Narasimhaswami's *Devotees' Experiences of Sai Baba*. Osborne appropriately pointed out that Narke made some generalizations (*The Incredible Sai Baba*, p. 115).

(71) For more on Gustadji, see notes 8 and 62 above.

(72) Sahukar, pp. 52–3.

(73) Whose identity survived in Osborne's account as a "Muslim saint" (p. 121).

(74) Osborne, p. 19; C.B. Purdom, *The Perfect Master* (1937), p. 26.

(75) According to Murphet, cited, pp. 22–3, acceptable concessions were made to the Muslim minority through the diplomacy of H.S. (Kaka) Dixit, a devotee who was a solicitor by profession. Cf. Osborne, p. 123.

(76) Kabir is reported to have died at Maghar, where a dispute arose between his Hindu and Muslim followers over the disposal of his body. Just when an appeal to arms seemed imminent, it was discovered that the corpse had changed into a heap of flowers. See Ahmad Shah, trans., *The Bijak of Kabir* (1917; repr. New Delhi: Asian Publication Services, 1979), p. 28.

(77) Satya Sai Baba of Puttaparti was born in 1926 and claimed in 1940 to be a reincarnation of the Shirdi master. Fame accrued very quickly. It is reported that he would produce ash (*udhi*) from thin air, and likewise photos of Sai Baba, and gerua cloth which he said was from the *kafni* which Sai Baba used to wear. See Murphet, cited, pp. 58 ff. It may be observed that photographs of the Shirdi adept were not difficult to obtain at that time, since Narasimhaswami's revivalist campaign had commenced. The devotees of Satya regard him as an *avatar*, and believe that the signs which mark an *avatar* are the *siddhis* or supernormal powers (*ibid.*, pp. 203–4).

PART TWO:

UPASNI MAHARAJ OF SAKORI

CHAPTER ONE

EARLY LIFE

The subject of this biography is not so well known as Sai Baba, though it should not for that reason be assumed that he was any the less important.

Kashinath Govindrao Upasni was born on 15th May, 1870, at Satana in the district of Nasik, then part of the Bombay Presidency. He was the second child of a brahmin couple called Govindshastri and Rukminabai. From his early days he evinced an uncommon affinity with anything that boded of the mystical. Sometimes he was found in a state of depression that was considered unexplainable, a state of mind for which his relatives did not know the remedy. At an early age he found himself alienated from mundane perspectives.

There was only one person with whom he found solace. This was his grandfather Gopalashastri, a man learned in the scriptures, and who led an austere life. In the past he had taken a vow of *sannyas* or renunciation, becoming an ascetic. It was from him that young Upasni received his early Vedantic training.

When he was seven years of age, his parents decided to send him to school. I have been unable to ascertain the exact nature of the curriculum, whether traditional or subject to Western influence, but whatever it was, the boy hated the institution. For him it was like going to prison, and to study there was equivalent to being heavily punished. The reason for this was not the disinclination of laziness, but reaction to the formal tuition based upon information-cramming. Indian philosophy and religion were not favoured in the Westernized curricula, and were reduced to an indoctrination format of rote-learning by the orthodox pundits. In contrast, his grandfather was able to interpret Hinduism as a living code of experience. At that early age, the rituals of the brahmins possessed meaning for Upasni, though later he outgrew this inheritance. Discourses on the Vedanta appear to have been his favourite form of tuition. The word Vedanta literally means "end of the Vedas," referring to the Upanishads, Sanskrit texts long preserved orally by the brahmins.

He is reported to have displayed rare qualities for a person of his age. On an occasion when his grandfather Gopalashastri was invited to attend a marriage ceremony, the elder was unable to be present, and so instead sent young Kashinath Upasni as his representative, accompanied by his mother Rukminabai. This was a high privilege for the boy, as his learned grandfather was held in great esteem in the neighbourhood; a seat was always reserved for the latter at all public and private functions. When Kashinath Upasni and his mother arrived at the marriage ceremony, the host requested him to occupy the seat reserved for Gopalashastri. But the boy declined to accept the honour, saying: "I am not as great as my grandfather; I do not deserve the honour which is his due." His humility did not pass unobserved, and one of the elders present said to him: "You are the cub of a lion. You will yourself become a lion."

As he grew up, Upasni became increasingly dissatisfied with the prospects of scholarship, social life, and Westernization. When scarcely twelve years of age, he resolved to enter a fresh field of experience as a wandering ascetic. His aim was to attain knowledge of the *Brahman*, the Vedantic Absolute, conceived not as a theoretical denominator but as a fact of experience in those capable of it. He left the shelter of his parental home and went on foot to the town of Nasik, one of the most famous places of pilgrimage in Western India. There he met an old friend of his grandfather's, who, when he had heard the boy's story, requested him to stay at his own residence in Nasik. The boy accepted the invitation, but disliked being a burden to his host. Though he lodged in the old man's house, he would not accept food from his host; instead he would go out and beg for food when hungry. When the father of Upasni received news that his son was in Nasik, he concocted a plan to retrieve him; the parent did not approve of his son living as a monk. Govindshastri sent a crafty telegram to say that Rukminabai was on her death-bed and pining to see him. Upon receipt of this message, the boy felt sorrow-stricken and decided to make his way back. When he arrived home however, he found his mother in her usual healthy condition. Disheartened at his father's ruse, he finally agreed to the persistent pleas of his parents to stay with them. But he remained heavy-hearted, and his yearning for the life of a *sannyasin* (renunciate) did not diminish.

Early marriage was a prevalent Hindu custom, and his elders pressurized him into matrimony with a girl named Durgabai. This event weighed upon his spirit more heavily than ever. But within a couple of years, his girl-wife passed away, a victim of the high mortality rate in India. His parents anxiously forced him into a second marriage at the age of sixteen, hoping to keep him occupied with mundane affairs. Again however, it produced no effect upon his temperament. He was painfully aware that his parents had chained him to a course of life abhorrent to his own directive. Daily he requested them to allow him the ochre robe of the mendicant, but although they registered his unhappiness, they still could not bring themselves to acquiesce to his wishes. They were taking the attitude, sanctioned by caste custom, that the life of the householder should precede that of the ascetic in old age; social customs are not proof of the best course in life for varying individuals.

As time passed, it became increasingly apparent that Kashinath Upasni would die of melancholy if events remained static. His parents were at last obliged, therefore, to give consent to his wishes. After obtaining their blessings, he bade goodbye to his family. Travelling to Poona, he applied himself to *sadhana* (a course of discipline).

For a number of years he underwent severe austerities, endeavouring to focus his concentrated attention upon an inner reality. He left Poona on foot, with the intention of finding a suitable spot for a secluded programme of *sadhana*. The culmination of these endeavours occurred in 1899, when he was almost thirty years of age. While resting in a temple about eight miles from Nasik, he espied a cave situated on the top of a hillside. He made his way to this cave, and finding it to his liking, he made his abode there. He remained a full year inside it, not stepping foot outside during this time. He was heedless of bodily functioning, taking no food (and no water, it is said) throughout the whole period. Experiencing a state of inner absorption, he detached himself from the level of normal needs. During this feat of protracted contemplation, he made contact with inner dimensions of consciousness. But when at length this illumination subsided, he felt drastically weak in body. He hauled himself out of the cave, reduced to a bare skeleton of skin and bones. Only a fraction of physical strength remained after such a lengthy interment, but he managed with difficulty and sheer force of will to return to the plains. There he came to the village of Gawalwadi, where the inhabitants fed him for about three months. It was a necessary interval of recuperation, and in return for their kindness, he tried to be of use to these villagers.

Persons who read of such meditative feats and set about trying to emulate them (increasingly rare nowadays) are not usually told of the difficulties involved. The changeover to normal physical function can be extremely critical, and can effectively hospitalize the unwary. Upasni was an exceptional *sadhaka* (one who practises *sadhana*) by all accounts, and often pushed himself to a limit that is normally unendurable.

He had undergone a powerful shock to his whole physical and mental system. He felt an urgent need to stabilize his faculties, and that he should see his family again. He therefore journeyed back on foot to Satana in July 1900. After the reunion, he stayed with his family for some while, but within three years he lost first his father, then his grandfather, and lastly his wife. Not wishing to be shackled again to matrimony, he then left home for a time in case his elders arranged another match. He came back a few months later, only to find that his mother and uncle wanted him to marry a girl who was of a similar mind to himself. The result of this recurrent situation was a third marriage for Upasni, only six months after the death of his second wife. He was not breaking any monastic rules, never having taken a formal vow of *sannyas*. A sufi pattern of balanced development was repeatedly making itself felt in his life-style.

It was now about the end of 1903, and subsequently he travelled with his new wife to Poona, where he lived at the home of his brother Balkrishna, who was then a professor at the Poona Training College. From here, after coming to an agreement with his wife, he proceeded alone to Sangli, not far from Kolhapur. In Sangli there is a shrine known as the Shri Dattaguru temple, on the banks of the Krishna River; in this sanctuary Upasni resided for two and a half years, living as an ascetic inmate. His lean diet consisted mainly of the leaves of certain trees; only occasionally did he partake of grains and fruits. His interest in the problems of nutriment for the physical organism led him to study the traditional Hindu science of the herbalist, but apart from this, nothing further is known of his experiences at that period.

Afterwards he set out for Poona again, where he rejoined his wife after being captured and put to work by a tough band of gypsies, one of the hazards of the rural backwater. Turning his attention to a means of livelihood for himself and his wife, he journeyed with her back to Satana. During his temple life at Sangli he had gathered a wide knowledge of Ayurvedic medicines, a subject which he had also studied in earlier years. At Satana, he now began to practise as an Ayurvedic doctor. This profession specialized in herbal and other remedies; it was an ancient medical science based on Vedic texts. Upasni rapidly achieved success, and became well known throughout the neighbourhood.

Enthusing over the prospects of establishing a hospital, with this aim in view he soon moved from Satana to Amraoti, situated near Nagpur in the Central Provinces. Shortly after arrival he founded a nursing-home which he named the Rama Ashram. He was an ideal doctor, giving free treatment to the poor, and being more concerned with restoring health than making money. It is not therefore surprising that he became extremely popular with the people of Amraoti. In addition to his other labours, he edited a medical magazine called *Bheshaja Ratnamala* for three years.

Although he had now achieved a very respectable social identity, he was unmoved by the change in status, and after a sojourn of about four years at Amraoti, events began to lose their savour for him. He now desired only to return to his days of seclusion and introspection. His wife had actively cooperated with him in everything he had accomplished, and in consultation with her he decided to end his career as a doctor, despite the accession of name and riches. Accordingly, they left together for places of pilgrimage.

Though he seems not to have known it at the time, Upasni was duplicating a sufi vocation which adopts alternate phases of a contemplative existence and social ballast. The person who follows this course is often extremely successful in their profession, business, or whatever other career it may be, but has to be prepared to relinquish it completely if necessary. Upasni's subsequent sufi teacher later indicated that he had been inwardly guiding the disciple's earlier life; this sounds fanciful to critics, but it is undeniable that Upasni's life pattern was atypical for Hindu ascetics.

Moving northwards to Ujjain, for many months he and his partner led a life of retirement here. Upasni spent the greater part of each day in meditation, trying to recapture the experiences he had undergone in the cave near Nasik. Once when they were staying at Omkareshwar, he entered a state of deep meditation in which his body received a sudden and violent shock, resulting in his losing consciousness of it. He not only completely stilled his mind in this condition, but also stopped breathing. His wife hastily roused him from this inert suspension by sprinkling water over him, afraid that her husband would die unless he took breath. But he found the act of breathing an extremely difficult and painful exercise; the vibratory impact of his experience had disturbed the normal functioning of the lungs. Instead, his respiratory process had to be engineered by the artificial movement of his stomach. This was the commencement of a lengthy breathing trouble.

Difficulties of this nature are usually induced by the

practice of *pranayama*, the yogic science of breath (which is only a science in the hands of an expert, and even then, only under very special conditions). But Upasni had not been undertaking any such exercises, and he could not at first understand what had happened. His normal physical rhythm had been disturbed by the intensity of his concentrative powers; prolonged meditation can have unpleasant side-effects that are not always allowed for by enthusiasts. The episode provides an example of what can happen to a pupil who has the capacity to prepare himself for the *lataif* process, but who lacks the necessary presence of an adept to make vital adjustments. Upasni had exceptional will-power and contemplative faculties, but beyond a certain point, he did not know how to use these abilities properly, the common plight of those outside a direct teaching situation.

The art of balance at each and every stage of the inner path is known in genuine sufi "schools," but is largely missing from "popular Sufism," and perhaps even more so from ascetic Vedanta and modern Yoga. The question of special ballast does not of course apply to those who do not or cannot connect with finer states of mind, since "balance" in mundane matters can then simply become an excuse for not making basic efforts, as is typical of fake schools and leisure aspirants.

The disruption of Upasni's breathing rhythm served as a shock factor which successfully deterred him from overintensive meditation at this juncture. It necessarily altered his plans, and as will be seen, resulted in events that would not otherwise have happened.

Since Upasni now wanted treatment for his breathing discomfort, he and his wife retraced their steps to Amraoti, from where they travelled to Nagpur after a few days. At that same time, Narayan Maharaj (d. 1945) happened to be staying in Nagpur on a brief visit; he was an increasingly well known entity of Western India. This sage had an ashram at Kedgaon, about thirty miles from Poona, and in his earlier years had been an itinerant sadhu. A brahmin by birth, Narayan was also in favour with brahmins owing to his patronage of ceremonial, but a number of other features set him apart from the average guru. He was a strange mixture of simple living habits and opulent attire. At his ashram, he was in the daily habit of retiring alone for several hours at a time into a special underground cell which had been constructed in accordance with his requirements.

No doctor was able to alleviate Upasni's respiratory trouble, but he did gain his first meeting with Narayan Maharaj, whom he ever afterwards respected. Upasni was but one among the many who wished for the *darshan* (meeting) of the sadguru, but Narayan beckoned him to sit near. The sadguru then garlanded Upasṇi with a wreath taken from his own neck. This was regarded by Upasni as a significant omen.

His breathing ailment persisted, and took an acute form when he subsequently moved south to Dhulia. The pain became so unbearable that he left his home alone to seek some form of remedy, and failing this, resolved to shed his mortal frame, which he now regarded as a vehicle of incessant torture.

It was then about the beginning of 1911, when our subject was forty years old, a sturdily built man of ascetic and scholarly inclinations whose horizons now seemed dark with the nemesis of afflicted breathing. Hoping to find a balm for his sufferings, he passed through Ahmednagar, an old city of the Deccan, and there heard of a yogi of Rahuri known as Kulkarni Maharaj. The latter was said to be unusually proficient in yogic and related practices, and so the traveller decided to go out of his way to visit this man. Rahuri is a town about twenty-five miles north of Ahmednagar, and there Kulkarni Maharaj not only received him cordially, but with his own hands applied oil to the visitor's body, and gave him a hot water bath in order to relax him. After a meal, the yogi strongly advised the visitor to seek out Hazrat Sai Baba of Shirdi, who lived about thirty miles north. But because Sai Baba was a Muslim, Upasni did not feel inclined to go to him, preferring instead to associate with persons of his own religious background. He said indignantly: "Why should I go to a Muslim and pay him homage? Even if I am likely to be benefited at his hands, I must not call upon him."

This was the conventional attitude of an orthodox brahmin, an attitude which did not befit his capacity of understanding, and which had to be eradicated in him the hard way.

That same evening at Rahuri, Upasni met an old man who advised him to drink only hot water in an effort to lessen the pain of his deficient breathing apparatus. This treatment did in fact later bring him considerable relief, but not just yet.

He took leave of his host after a few days, proceeding into the nearby jungle. Unmindful of the thorns and other numerous discomforts, he lived in this grim environment for several days. His psychological state was one of acute frustration. There was depression over his breathing difficulties, poisoned by the conviction that he was soon to die. He was upset that his *sadhana* had been interrupted, since he had lost the inner poise he had acquired, and his consciousness had instead been wrenched outwards once more. Death seemed to him to be preferable to the limbo of daily existence.

Upasni did not really want to emerge alive from his jungle setting. He felt oppressed and constricted beyond endurance. Ever since his childhood, he had struggled for the supreme state of consciousness specified in the Vedanta, and of which he had at times gained fragmentary experience sufficient to goad him on when many would stop. Time and again he had been pulled back, it seemed. How long would it all have to go on? If death was the solution, then let it be death.

It was either here, or very shortly after, that he centralized in his mind the impulse to seek out his fellow brahmin Narayan Maharaj for specific guidance, a highly positive incentive that urged him along a route towards distant Kedgaon. Though he had seen the sadguru already, he now felt that there must be far more potential in the contact.

Painfully but determinedly, he made his way south to the villages of Jejuri and Morgaon, and from there to Supa, where he stopped to rest in a temple for some days. The people of Supa were impressed with the qualities he showed, and to his embarrassment they paid him homage as a saint.

He told them repeatedly that he was an ordinary itinerant *sadhaka*, but whatever he said, the would-be followers still presented themselves. He did not allow himself to be sidetracked by the adulation showered upon him, but quickly moved on to Kedgaon.

Upasni did not possess a devotional temperament, and does not appear to have formerly taken a strong interest in becoming the disciple of a guru. He tended to be fiercely independent, relying on his own efforts. But now he had found that his own efforts were insufficient to solve looming problems.

Arriving at Kedgaon, he found that Narayan Maharaj had gone to Bombay, a considerable distance away. But undaunted, he quickly turned his pain-wracked steps in that direction. When he reached his destination, he successfully located the sage, whom he found in company. Upasni expressed a desire to speak privately, and Narayan told him to come back in the evening. When the visitor returned at the time stipulated, the sage immediately said to him: "Do not be afraid. Everything will be alright in a few days."

Narayan then gave Upasni a roll of *pan* (betel-leaf) from a silver box which he kept for this commodity. *Pan* is a common masticatory in India; the silver box was a typical characteristic of Narayan Maharaj, whose opulence concealed a simple and demanding lifestyle that he did not wish to share with all and sundry. The sage told his visitor to chew the *pan* thoroughly. The recipient knew that any such gift had a relevance, however simple it might appear. He was more unprepared for the sadguru's subsequent statements: "You have been thoroughly painted inside and outside. Now nothing remains. Today you have been so painted as till now nobody was ever painted."

Upasni was puzzled by these words, and at the time was unable to grasp their meaning. One might construe that both his inner and outer life had reached a climactic point of development. The symbolism was that of the application of paint to the face during religious ceremonies and initiations. The last sentence indicated that Narayan had performed for the visitor something very special which he had so far not bestowed upon anyone else.

"Never mind if you do not understand me," continued Narayan. "The time will come, and it is approaching fast, when you will understand everything." It was a bewildered Upasni who heard these words. Narayan then added more enigmatically: "For the present, be contented with believing that you have been thoroughly painted. I cannot explain what I mean."

Upasni departed in a quandary. It was evident that the sage would not tell him anything more. There was no clear advice as to what to do. He felt an impulse to go back to Rahuri.

On the following day, he again went to the sadguru and asked his permission to leave Bombay. Narayan replied: "You may go from Bombay whenever you like. I will meet you within a few days, and in such a way that I will permanently stay with you."

At these further words of mystery, Upasni continued to wonder at the significance of these disclosures.

Travelling back to Rahuri, he visited Kulkarni Maharaj for the second time. The yogi again urged him to present himself before Sai Baba of Shirdi. Upasni was evidently subconsciously prepared for the next move; this time he cast aside his prejudices and decided to act upon the advice, which was clear and unenigmatic.

He moved quickly on to Shirdi, arriving on the morning of 27th June, 1911. He made his way to the mosque to present himself before Sai Baba; his impressions of this event escaped record. In the afternoon he went for a bath, and afterwards joined the other Hindus in the performance of the *arati* ceremony. Then he took his meal, returning to the sufi in the evening, wishing to secure permission to leave Shirdi. But Sai Baba exclaimed: "What! Do you want to go away so soon? No, no, you shall not leave so soon. Go and stay for a few days in that yard."

The Vedantin was doing his best to regard the sufi as just another wayside holy man. He excused himself by saying that he wished to attend to some domestic affairs. Sai Baba replied with an air of finality: "If you must go, come back in eight days." Upasni said that he was very doubtful of being able to accomplish this, and then departed.

From Shirdi he moved six miles to Kopargaon, and there visited a Hindu saint called Brahmachari Bua. The latter asked him if he had been to Shirdi, and Upasni replied that he had taken the *darshan* of Sai Baba. The saint then told him that his visit to Shirdi had not served its purpose, and urged him to retrace his steps. But Upasni was determined instead to stay at a temple in Kopargaon, and accordingly took up residence there for a few days, frequently visiting Brahmachari Bua. One day the saint pressed him again to return to Shirdi, and while talk continued on this subject, a group of visitors drew up in a *tonga* (horse-cab). They wanted the *darshan* of the saint, and told him that they intended afterwards to visit Sai Baba. When they heard that Upasni had been to Shirdi, they not only pressed him to accompany them, but also offered to pay his *tonga* fare. Upasni seemed strangely reluctant to go, but finally yielded to the wishes of everyone present. It was particularly difficult for him to over-rule the request of a Hindu saint; he seems to have been practically pitting his will against Sai Baba.

The *tonga* reached Shirdi in the afternoon, and when the travellers alighted, they entered the rural mosque. After they had paid their respects, the sufi asked Upasni, "How many days have passed since you left the village?" Reviewing the matter, the visitor found to his surprise tht he had returned exactly on the eighth day, just as the adept had bidden. "Today is the eighth day, sir" he replied, and Sai Baba reminded him that he had not thought a return possible within this time limit. Upasni commented in admiration: "Baba, your ways of working are incomprehensible to me."

This event served to topple the scales, causing the visitor's initial guardedness to evaporate. He now decided to live under the personal orders of the sufi, who told him to make his abode in the same yard formerly stipulated. Upasni obeyed, though spending much of his time in Sai Baba's company, observing him more closely and keeping a keen eye on the daily occurrences. As a brahmin who was not averse to the more simple rituals, he took part in the *arati* ceremony that occurred in the mosque, but had the capacity to view this rite in a non-devotional perspective. During his eventful life, he had applied himself to practically every mode of the diverse Hindu tradition: the ritualistic, the devotional, the ascetic, yogic practices, the discriminatory path of *jnana* (knowledge) with its emphasis upon non-dualism (advaita). He was now to find all these experiential threads converging in, and superceded by, his new training.

There is no further reference to his breathing trouble.

He had good cause to remember the recent words of Narayan Maharaj: "I will meet you within a few days, and in such a way that I will permanently stay with you." At the time these words were spoken, Upasni could not have foretold that he would be enrolling as a resident pupil of Sai Baba. It was startling indication of an identity in awareness between these gurus of high grade, regardless of their cultural differences. Both of them can justifiably be distinguished by the Sanskrit term *sadguru*, which means a highly qualified teacher, and which anciently appears to have specified a different grade to gurus in general.

After a few days had passed, the sufi suddenly asked his new pupil for alms, not specifying any amount. Upasni brought to him only one rupee, which had turned black and green with age. When he submitted it, Sai Baba remarked: "Look at the kind of coin he has given me. From the rupees he has with him, he has deliberately selected a discoloured one." The chastened Upasni replied: "Baba, kindly return it to me, and I will bring another one for you." But Sai Baba said, "I *did* want a dark rupee, so let it remain." But when Upasni left the mosque to go for a meal, he felt extremely uncomfortable over this incident, and returned to his teacher with the best-looking coin he had in his possession. "It was a great mistake of mine to have given you the dark rupee," he said when presenting the new one. The sufi again accepted, and rubbed the coin against a cloth to increase the lustre of the metal. But the episode was not over, for at that juncture a Hindu devotee named Haribhau Choubal entered the mosque and presented Sai Baba with a gift of several rupees. The sufi promptly asked the newcomer for more, but he had none extra with him. Sai Baba then requested Choubal to return to his residence nearby and bring back any money he could find on the premises. Upasni took this as a cue, and himself offered to bring all the money he had at his disposal. He went quickly to his abode and brought back his entire fund of rupees and some additional small change, presenting the total amount to Sai Baba. He was now left destitute, and thereafter depended upon the sufi for physical sustenance. He threw in his lot in a similar manner to Gustadji Hansotia.

Prior to the performance of *arati*, it was Sai Baba's habit to utter a series of statements that were intelligible only to those individuals to whom they were directed. Upasni discovered that many of these references were detailed descriptions of his own past history, and were specifically intended for him alone.

Several months passed. Upasni became alarmed at his complete material dependence upon his teacher, as it was against his principles to be a financial burden. For this reason he considered obtaining Sai Baba's permission to leave Shirdi. A Hindu pupil named Madhavrao Deshpande had come to be regarded as the general spokesman in such matters, and so Upasni tried to gain the sufi's sanction through this intermediary. But each time Deshpande brought up the subject, Sai Baba said that permission would be given "after settling all the accounts," giving no explanation of his meaning.

One day Upasni and Deshpande were both engaged in massaging the feet of Sai Baba, and Deshpande took the opportunity to broach once more the topic of permission to leave. This time Sai Baba gave a more extensive reply, speaking of Upasni in the following strain: "Listen carefully to what I am saying about him. He has to stay here not for one year or even one year and a half. He has to stay here for four years. After four years, the grace of Mahalsapati (a god of the Hindu pantheon) will fall upon him, and all his accounts will be clear. He should stay quietly in Vithoba's temple for four years. He has a very good future. There are none like him; such is his worth. The whole world is on one side, and he is on the other . . . He should stay quietly in Vithoba's temple, and I will do what I want to."

It is known that Upasni felt unworthy of the destiny the

sufi had spoken of. He continued to ask permission to leave Shirdi. The temple which the adept referred to was a short distance from Shirdi; the reason for this emphasis was not at all apparent at the time, even though Upasni had for long been accustomed to residing in temples.

The situation was fast approaching a climax. Sai Baba now gave intimations of a different nature to anything previous. On one occasion he said to Upasni: "Now you should not worry about anything. I am fully conscious of your worth. For many years I have been after you. Whatever good or bad actions have until now been performed by you, have really been done by me. You were not conscious of me, but I was fully aware of you. For years I have been thinking of you in my heart. Now there is nowhere to go or to come. If you are unable to do anything, do not do anything."

Then in language symbolic of the service which he was soon to render, the sufi stated further: "I will myself purchase the ticket for you and will, with my own hands, seat you in the train; and without allowing the train to stop anywhere, I will take you straight to where I want to take you."

Upasni listened soberly to all this with his head bent towards his chest. He said nothing.

CHAPTER TWO

AT KHANDOBA'S TEMPLE

It was now approximately early 1912. At the sufi's continual prompting, Upasni made his abode in the temple earlier referred to. It was actually known as Khandoba's temple, though Sai Baba always referred to it as "Vithoba's" (Vithoba is an epithet of Vishnu the Preserver). This small stone edifice was in a relatively isolated position outside Shirdi, and seems to have been disused and in a state of decay. It fulfilled the requirements of a special solitude, since Sai Baba now wanted Upasni at a distance from the general file of devotees and visitors.

News arrived that year of how Upasni's wife had died of illness. His link with the outside world was no more. He did not dwell on personal sorrow, since he had seen death in its deeper perspective.

During the crucial interval occurring since his inner absorption had been interrupted by respiratory stress, Upasni had evidently progressed to a higher state by an unexpectedly difficult route. He was now to reap the full rewards of his thirty years struggle. Sai Baba had indicated that Upasni was unique insofar as his own activity was concerned.

Upasni became the recipient of the full impact of the sufi's *baraka.* What he now embarked upon was not a *sadhana*, but a phase of complete inner activation that was directly imparted to him by the Shirdi adept. Upasni had been thoroughly prepared for the *lataif* process in its most powerful form, and was to be heir to the experiences his teacher had undergone many years before.

It was because he directly experienced this process that he ever afterwards refused to speak of it in the popular *kundalini* terminology. He knew that the texts and surviving traditions upon which it was based were only hints, indications, symbolic outlines, and even unwitting misrepresentations of an ancient truth which mankind is largely unprepared for.

It should not be expected that any genuine "school" will hand out the details of this process, since it is an experiential and not a descriptive matter. It does not occur to many present day readers that compilers of old texts were as ignorant of the true workings of the process as the modern exponents are.

Western students can become easily excited at hearing of chakras, coiled serpents and the like, particularly if the exponent can abort some sexual symbolism from his material. Playful versions of the Taoist equivalent were for long current in China, and exert the same fascination for the vulgarists of other cultures also. The scientifically minded observer might well conclude from the differences inherent in the Taoist, Buddhist, and Hindu versions, the Western derivatives, and the less well known sufi versions, that some of these are incorrect or very incomplete.

Many of those struggling to "raise their *kundalini*" ought perhaps to be told that they have been duped into a sheer waste of time (and money) by commercial literature or classes, for the simple reason that there is as yet nothing substantial enough to "raise," and further, nothing strongly enough formed to take it to. It is rather like banging one's head against a locked door instead of going to find the key.

If by chance, those with more forward capacities were to become "accidentally" magnetized to a partial spurt of the underlying process, they run the risk of becoming cut off from their normal layer of awareness, or at the very least, incurring a severe psychic shock. A copyist teacher or commercial guru has no chance of helping them if any difficulty should occur. Fortunately perhaps, difficulties rarely occur in the West owing to the general thick-skinned receptivity of the practitioners, but in the East there are dangers known to those genuine yogis and others who dislike tourists.

There has, providentially enough, as yet been no Occidental fad for the Indian practice of continual gazing at the sun. The rarer type of yogi has been copied in this by umpteen others. Since the white-skinned race is partial enough to a drastic change of skin colour in leisure hours during the hotter weather, there is no explicit reason for assuming that we will not as yet see any such fad. If it does ever occur, then hopefully any best-selling books on the subject will not forget to state that many of the copyist practitioners of India were stricken with blindness, many partially so, but some completely.

An instance of the authentic activation process occurred at an unimposing temple near Shirdi. There were no books involved, no charts or diagrams, no course of instruction, no explicit references to the process itself, no weird and wonderful terminology of any kind. When it was finished, there was no remnant symbol material left lying about to be ill-digested by self-seeking teachers and gullible students.

When Kashinath Upasni made his abode in the derelict Khandoba's temple, he spent most of his time alone and behind closed doors. He went daily to see Sai Baba only at the hour of the *arati* ceremony. After a while the sufi told him that it was not necessary for him to come every day.

A change was observed to come over him. His acute introspection was obvious, but there was more than this, an indefinable emanation.

At first he took food every day at a particular house in the vicinity. Finally however, it was made clear by the occupants that he was not welcome anymore. But instead of going elsewhere, he ceased to eat food altogether. Furthermore, he no longer went to Sai Baba's mosque. Instead he remained alone in his temple as if the world no longer existed.

Anxious pupils of Sai Baba and curious villagers found a visual spectacle awaiting them. The interior of the shrine was notable for its filth, and was infested by snakes and scorpions. Its human occupant seemed oblivious of his environment. His body was extremely thin owing to lack of food, and his pulse beat unusually slowly. Yet his face consistently appeared fresh and radiant, as if lit from within.

It was remembered that on one of the last occasions when

Upasni had visited the mosque, Sai Baba had said to him: "I have filled all existence. Wherever you see, there is none but me." Devotees had interpreted this as one of the sufi's general statements of gnosis. Some of the more discerning pupils now grasped that Upasni was participating in the same "God-realization." He certainly did not advertise this, instead being acutely remote and aloof, as if dead to his surroundings.

Later, Upasni briefly described an essential of his experience at this time. He said that some extrusion of a finer-than-physical energy arose from his head like the contents of a syringe, soaring high into the atmosphere and piercing the external sheath of the universe, becoming unified with a principle at once transcendent of form and yet immanent in it.

He ventured only a brief description because the shattering quality of such experiences can never be communicated; all minds lacking such experience form a pattern of associations which are far removed from the reality. There can be no substitute for the effort made to achieve the objective oneself.

A more easily understood framework of reference was Upasni's subsequent symbolical narration of the dual aspects of the false self (*nafs*) which are transcended during the *lataif* process. He saw two circles, in one of which an evil person exactly resembling himself was being dealt a sound thrashing by Sai Baba, and subsequently thrown onto a burning pyre. In the other circle he saw Sai Baba pointing out a virtuous person, again of the same likeness to himself, who was seated comfortably upon a heap of rupees. "He is the good one, and the other was an evil one. Then who am I?" he asked the sufi. Sai Baba replied: "You are beyond both of these; you and I are one, and all this wealth belongs to us."

The new candidate for masterhood did not communicate such references just yet however. His own successor later asserted that Upasni gained the realization at this time of what is known in sufi lore as *fana-fillah*, and for some while afterwards possessed only a slight degree of outer awareness, prior to the arduous stabilization which follows the drastic opening-up of hitherto dormant areas of inner consciousness.

At the risk of mixing terminologies, one might imagine an atomic explosion occurring in the consciousness, destroying the limiting structure of mental impressions, with the important qualification that the person who develops enough resistance to the fall-out becomes immune to the effects of radioactivity. There is an old Hindu tradition that the physical organism usually expires three days after the achievement of *nirvikalpa samadhi*, the "inconceptual realization." This is the equivalent Hindu term for *fana-fillah*, though nowadays used extremely loosely; most proclaimed instances of it are more comparable to a sparkler than an atomic bomb.

The popular Indian idea of *samadhi*, now current in the West, extends only to the limited reaches of *savikalpa*, the lesser *samadhi*. There are many such inferior states, which it is necessary to speedily pass beyond, since they can delude the subject into thinking that he has gained the ultimate. *Nirvikalpa* is much more rare than is often believed, and is quite frequently mistakenly extolled as the final goal.

The myopic idea of the "master" who is more or less permanently immersed in unconsciousness of the world around him is deserving of opprobrium (a confused variant of this is ordinary human consciousness alternating with supposed *nirvikalpa*). Lesser men of the path may have such a state, but the favoured tag of "master" is a misnomer in such cases. A distinction was made in the old Sanskrit formula of *sahaj samadhi*, the "natural" *samadhi* which surpasses that of *nirvikalpa* by fully equilibrizing in the world of matter. Even then a man of *sahaj* may not be a "master" in the lofty sense ascribed to the term, since *sahaj samadhi* is equivalent to the sufic *baqa-billah*, which is not the ultimate grade of attainment. The Hindu tradition does not clearly delineate the various states and stages, and popular Sufism has made cheapened usage of equivalent terminology. (Meher Baba's emphasis upon the term *sadguru* in alignment with *qutub* was an unusual attempt to give some operationalized meaning to such vintage but now sadly jumbled terms).

Upasni's unofficial fast continued month after month. Pupils of Sai Baba begged him to eat, but he ignored all entreaties. They brought plates of food for him and left these near him; it was stray dogs and crows who consumed these offerings. If pressed to partake of anything, he was liable to be violent; he would throw away the food, and shower abuse upon those concerned. His responses did in fact discourage visitors in general. Such events are not the fare of tourism.

The acute abstinence continued for over a year. His sturdy frame was reduced to a skeletal appearance, but the radiance continued. Finally a prominent pupil of Sai Baba approached Upasni with the insistent news that the master himself had ordered that he should take some food. Only now did the transformed one comply, taking some coffee and a little solid food. It seems apparent that this event marked a new inner movement in his consciousness with regard to stabilization in the physical world.

It was not long before Sai Baba gave another order for Upasni to live on water only, to which the latter just as readily complied. It was puzzling in view of Upasni's lean condition. Further, not everyone connected the two instances when Sai Baba began to eat large quantities of food contrary to his usual habit. Yet despite his adequate repasts, the sufi would often complain that he was feeling very hungry.

It seems that Upasni was not merely undergoing the transition from *fana* to *baqa*; he was assisting also in a project or projects undertaken by his initiator. These special projects can and do involve denial and stress on the part of the elect.

Though Upasni remained a physical skeleton for the moment, it was intended only as a passing phase and not as any ascetic ideal of the kind sometimes unperceptively perpetuated. Adulators of this ideal have yet to grasp that the really advanced examples of it may be in a state of realigning with the world around them, not escaping from it.

Various persons who approached in the hope of *darshan*

were warded off with abuse. Yet he could also show forbearance when pestered by children and other ignorant entities. The neighbouring villagers came to regard him as a great holy man, and accordingly held the precincts of the temple in veneration.

Owing to the schism between his inner consciousness and his cognizance of externals, he was prone to unbalanced behaviour, sometimes acting like a "madman," to use one description. He was responding to two opposite sets of stimuli and the resultant discordancy to which he could not as yet adapt.

On one occasion he embraced the body of a dead horse near the temple, and remained the whole day with the carcase, even though it was being steadily devoured by hungry birds of prey. One interpretation is that he was aware of the divine essence behind the form, that he knew that the "soul" of the horse still lived, that "dead" matter is an illusion.

As he made increasing linkage with the world around him, he would sometimes leave the temple and help peasants with their manual labour. Frail though he was, he seemed to revel in the sweat and muscular movement. This was because the intensive physicalization served to redistribute relevant energies governing the subtle centres (*lataif*), helping the consciousness to shift focus, though very gradually in this most delicate of all "initiatory" occurrences.

There was one occasion when he personally bathed a leper and also washed the dirty clothes of this unfortunate. It was a striking prelude to his emerging role of service. It is relevant to add that to people of his grade, all others are lepers, however desirable they might imagine themselves to be.

Mere recounting of his visible actions can give no idea of the intricacy of his inner range which had broken all normal psychological boundaries defined by impressions (*sanskaras*). He described several experiences at this period, though they should be taken as fragmentary aspects of a whole. He was aware, he said, of the physical world revolving about him, while he was simultaneously outside the revolving sphere of matter, stretched into infinity in this greater self. He said also that he experienced this vortex of matter to gradually decrease in size until it vanished altogether.

There were times when he evidenced seeing objects and places that were a long distance away, his extended perception acting as a kind of close-up lens. In contrast to this, one afternoon he was sensitive for some while to what he described as an engulfing darkness that blotted out the sun, though the solar orb was emitting its usual glare at the time. These variations were due to the expansions and contractions of his spatio-temporal awareness, which was a fluctuating *addition* to his permanent experience of ultra-dimensional reality.

Sufis have termed this state of fluctuation of the outer consciousness as *fana-ma-al-baqa*, the halfway point between the two major stages indicated.

There were other experiences he spoke of concerning "circles of light" of varying dimensions. These he perceived as approaching him and being absorbed into him. In these ethereal photospheres he viewed events and people, including deceased persons he had known in the past. One event of particular importance he described as an extensive meeting of saints and adepts of the past and present, an assembly occurring upon the inner planes of consciousness. They were concerned with a crucial matter that had some bearing upon world affairs, and were awaiting the presence of Sai Baba before crystallizing the formative energies they were about to release. Some decision had to be passed. When Sai Baba appeared with an illuminate of Christian background, the decision was finalized.

These varying fragments of special awareness were heard at this time by Upasni's earliest pupils. They were actually pupils of Sai Baba, who now told them to regard Upasni as their own teacher from now on. Their number was by no means large, and it seems that Sai Baba drafted them over to his chargeman at intervals, some at a slightly later date. Most of them seem to have retained their connection with Shirdi for a while. The identities are now largely lost with time. One was the Zoroastrian Gustadji Hansotia, another was Dr. Pillai, a Hindu. This latter was a frequent visitor to Khandoba's temple, and to him Upasni predicted the First World War in 1913, one year before it commenced.

Most of Sai Baba's followers did not grasp the importance of the temple dweller. Some felt that he might be a saint of some sort perhaps. Some regarded him merely as a *sadhaka*, some were completely unaware of him. The element of non-interest was possibly due to some extent to the general difficulty experienced in approaching Upasni, who was apt to be ferociously unsociable. It was also strongly influenced by that aspect of the devotee mentality which closely resembles that of old retainers. Pupils who had been with Sai Baba for a number of years liked to think that Upasni was of little or no consequence because he was a comparative newcomer. After all, *they* had been with the master for so much longer. And furthermore, Upasni did not even see Sai Baba anymore.

A somewhat comical case of such non-understanding was afforded by one Dadasaheb Khaparde. This Hindu devotee stayed at Shirdi for a while, and for some reason took it into his head to go and talk to Upasni concerning mystical subjects. That is, he persisted in voicing his explanations of these subjects. Upasni did not seem inclined to listen to him, but unperturbed, the visitor graciously aired his loquacity, possibly mistaking silence for attentiveness.

Upasni's fast on water lasted for about three years. At its close he had achieved the necessary balance in consciousness, fitting the requirements of *baqa*. He was referred to by his pupils as Maharaj ("great king"), a common appellation bestowed on holy men. He was more rarely known as Baba. It was now about the end of 1915.

To Gustadji Hansotia, Sai Baba explained: "I have given Maharaj everything. Whatever he is, he is mine. There is no spiritual difference between him and me. Mine alone has been the responsibility for the perfection which is his today."

Many years later, after Upasni's death, his disciple Meher Baba said of the former's stay at Khandoba's temple: "Maharaj was the only one there who knew who Sai Baba really was. Maharaj himself was so great that if his grace were to descend on a particle of dust, it would be transformed into God." This might sound poetic to some readers, but there is no doubt that Upasni was an unusually vibrant entity in the annals of Vedanta and Yoga.

CHAPTER THREE

A HINDU HERCULES

According to sufi lore, a teaching master will often appoint several deputies (*khalifas*), i.e., disciples who gain the prerogative of teachers. But he can only appoint one chargeman, one successor in office. None of these appointments go around with placards about their necks advertising that such and such a master has given them a mandate. Nor is the master himself under any obligation to make a public proclamation.

As a rule, these appointments are only interested in direct contact with those who are teachable in terms of an inner development. They might not allow anyone to recognize their authority unless they deem that person eligible to become a pupil.

Having completed the prescribed period of four years at Khandoba's temple, Upasni quietly left Shirdi at the beginning of 1916. He departed at midnight for the town of Shindi, accompanied by a Dr. Ganapatrao. The only other person who knew of his departure was Dr. Pillai, aforementioned, who saw him off. The latter remained in Shirdi but kept a close secret as to the whereabouts of his teacher. When people asked Sai Baba concerning this sudden disappearance, the sufi would say that Dr. Pillai had concealed Maharaj.

Upasni had to leave in order to establish his own work; the chargeman's course of action usually entails a complete break from the home centre.

This disappearance seemed further proof to the weaker devotee mentality that Upasni was not one of the fold. Comprising as they did the lowest psychological focus which Sai Baba allowed to form around him, they were the least susceptible to any inner change, and likewise to any development in the teaching situation itself. This is a common feature of any large scale human grouping associated with a living adept. The general outlook is not always devotional of course, but in India this particular disposition is usually uppermost. It is this comparatively static element which cannot adjust when the time arrives, and who carry on after the exemplar's death as though he were still alive, and as though other exemplars do not exist.

Meanwhile at Shindi, Dr. Ganapatrao engaged the services of a civil surgeon in order to perform an operation that Upasni was in need of. The ailment was haemorroids, and the operation was simple enough, but Upasni consented to it on the condition that he would not take chloroform. A simple operation therefore became an extremely painful process. Although he was given no sedative, he remained quiet and still throughout the operation, astounding the surgeon by his detachment from bodily pain.

For a few weeks afterwards he stayed quietly at Shindi, his physique filling out once more after his protracted abstinence. Dr. Ganapatrao had a brother known as Chinnaswami who lived in distant Bengal, and this man invited Upasni to stay at his home in Kharagpur, a town in the Monghyr district. Upasni consented, but forbid his host to disclose his past history to anyone in the neighbourhood. He did not wish to be swamped by people wishing for the usual *darshan*.

When he arrived in this north-eastern corner of the country, his new host tried hard to conceal all details of the guest's identity. But Upasni's presence seemed to exert a magnetic influence, and scarcely a week had elapsed before large numbers were pressing their visits upon him. The local people surrounded him at every opportunity, and his fame quickly became widespread throughout the district. However, it was not to be the general round of *darshan*, for he quickly set about giving events an unexpected twist.

Traditional Hindu society, then far more so than now, is a complex of four castes. As is now widely known, the lowest stratum (*chandalas* or *mahars*) has no caste at all, existing outside the social system and regarded as "untouchables" by the orthodox brahmins. Upasni was himself a brahmin, but he acted as if the caste system had never been invented.

The reader who is still imagining our subject as an ascetic skeleton should now dispense with the idea. He had regained his former muscular physique, and was now a dynamo of outgoing energy. He wore rags which could have been taken for the garb of a beggar, aptly enough in view of his partiality for the socially downtrodden. The skeletal temple dweller now became a Hindu hercules, formerly in isolation but now active in the midst of society.

Devotees who came for *darshan*, expecting to find him sitting serenely cross-legged and giving discourses on lofty subjects, instead found him helping workmen in the streets, his face glistening with sweat just like those of his companions. His vigorous course of action was not confined to roadworkers however, but to many other departments of labour that fell to the lot of the poverty-sticken. The more lowly the work was, the more he seemed to take zest in it. He would laboriously break up stones for the roads, he would help poor women to grind corn, and even participated in kitchen affairs by scouring the cooking vessels. The cobblers have always been some of the most destitute of Indian tradesmen, and he would sit with them and assist in mending footwear.

For centuries many untouchables had worked as menial sweepers or *bhangis*, the only calling upon to them, and considered (not without reason) the worst job in the social scale. Upasni now toiled as one of these, though it was considered unthinkable for a brahmin to perform the duties of a *bhangi*. With typical vigour he cleaned the foul-smelling streets of the slums and the shabby hovels which passed as houses. The *bhangi* did not simply sweep, since the job involved disposing of that human waste which is more of a problem when there is no sanitation.

Upasni was undertaking a special project involving social work, though from an angle that was not merely humanitarian. Such projects may be far more specialized than a teaching role as usually understood. This does not mean to say that some form of verbal teaching is not appended.

To climax the situation insofar as his new followers were

concerned, it was not long before Upasni moved from the abode of the affluent Chinnaswami to the very humble residence of a *bhangi*. Here lived Namdev Mahar and his wife Bhagubai, who were both devoted to him. This hovel was in the untouchable quarter of Kharagpur, where no caste Hindu would set foot as a rule. But men and women of social standing capitulated to this tactic, and entered the primitive dwelling of Namdev Mahar for the privilege of Upasni's *darshan*. Others followed suit in large numbers, and an intermingling of brahmins and *bhangis* became a common sight. It is difficult for the Westerner to understand the full psychological intricacies of this, since brahmins had long ago concocted the superstition that they would "lose caste" by associating with the outcastes. The roots of this belief go very far back in time, to the Vedic India of the Aryan settlers.

Upasni sometimes tested the scruple of his brahmin devotees by saying: "You belong to the highest caste. Are you not ashamed to approach me when I am staying with these untouchables?"

The reply would be: "Why should we be ashamed to come near you? Are you not *Paramatman*? To whatever place you go, it becomes holy. Wherever you go, we shall follow." *Paramatman* is a Sanskrit word meaning "Supreme Self," and here referred to the realization of *Brahman* with which he was now credited.

Many caste Hindus came to visit him every day in this previously detested locality. His inspiration moved some of the richer devotees to give large public feasts for all and sundry. From the viewpoint of Upasni, the existing social conditions had to alter before the real teaching could manifest more openly.

He seemed very much at home in his squalid surroundings. This depressed, illiterate section of the community did not pretend to know anything, they did not assume airs and graces, and practised no mock humility. Their simple devotion was very genuine, however quaint it may seem to the modern. In short, they lacked the veneer of falsity that comprises much civilization.

His mode of living at this period should be viewed in

relation to his deprecation of the social etiquette that was an effective barrier to wider social and psychological perspectives. He became noted for his complete indifference to bodily comfort and caste niceties of any kind, living in a basic manner that was in harmony with the worst of *bhangi* conditions. He went about naked, and sat or lay down in the most uncommodious of surroundings. After initially preparing his own food at Kharagpur, he had subsequently taken to begging at a few houses. Any food offerings he would collect in broken pieces of an earthen pot, which he would not part with for a new one. After a meal, he would wash the fragments of this disabled receptacle. But these same pieces of earthenware he would also use for the lofty function of relieving himself of his waste products. Shocked observers would watch him industriously wash the pieces clean again before collecting more food.

This indifference to hygiene was not something he intended to be copied in any way (for one thing, ignorance of basic hygiene was already a feature of *bhangi* life). In making himself seem the very untouchable of untouchables, he was attempting to lessen the gap between orthodox horror of the slovenly underdog (who handled filth all day) and the beginning of a new attitude to the social crime.

The insistence upon the less appealing aspect of life was carried over into a basic verbal emphasis to which he largely limited his "teaching": the divine is in everything, good or bad, beautiful or ugly, clean or unclean. He preferred to illustrate this in life episodes rather than repeat it *ad nauseam*. His main opportunity for this was gained in those incessant instances where devotees wished to worship him in the traditional Hindu manner. Instead of allowing them to worship his own person, he would improvise some symbol for the purpose. For example, one day while he was assisting a gang of workmen and wielding a hammer, a group of devotees arrived upon the scene, wishing to perform his *arati-puja*. He promptly asked them to worship the hammer. On another occasion, he responded to a similar request by presenting some woman with a torn shoe as an object of devotion. At one time, he not infrequently diverted such persistent attention to a primitive brick toilet which he used. It remains to be said that not everyone understood in these situations exactly what he was getting at. The hammer, for instance, meant application to relieving the lot of the workmen, the torn shoe was a pointer to the cobblers who worked for next to nothing, the noxious toilet would have to be cleaned out by some *bhangi* (in this case himself). In short, he was telling his compatriots to attend to present day needs, something that they actually saw him engaged in, rather than forever pestering him with anachronistic rites.

This man of vigour was quite unpredictable to average intelligence. A visitor once arrived with an artistically carved sandalwood chair, intending that the guru should sit upon it while receiving worship. Upasni made him burn the chair, and furthermore, throw his worship offering onto the fire thus created. It was only then that the guru gave the visitor his blessing.

Extremely forthright though he was on the whole, there was a softer aspect to his nature which he sometimes exhibited in cases of unclogged receptivity. One such case was that of a ten year old Maratha girl named Mira, to whom he would relate stories of instruction. Years later when she fell seriously ill, she made her husband take her all the way to Upasni's ashram at Sakori, preferring to die there in his proximity.

It was not only Hindus who were drawn to him at Kharagpur. There were hundreds of Muslim visitors in addition to the thousands of Hindus, and there were also some scores of Indian Christians. He occasionally visited the living-quarters of these Christian converts, and was known to talk to them on the subject of the spiritual path. Once he went to a local mosque and lay down there for a while; it was a strange habit of his to suddenly recline thus, as though temporarily severing himself from his surroundings.

There was a man at Kharagpur known as Chandu Baba (religious background unreported and possibly not known), who was locally regarded as a *siddha* or advanced being. He was evidently aware of Upasni's inner stature, for he unfailingly directed people to visit the newcomer. On one occasion Upasni and Chandu Baba met upon the road, and while they gazed at each other, the latter made a characteristic gesture of transferring his loin-cloth to his shoulders. These two practically naked men stood looking at each other for some time, but without saying a word. They continued upon their separate ways in silence. The meeting seemed to have significance; in both Sufi and Vedantic lore, the higher mystics are not dependent upon a verbal interchange. Later to his devotees, Upasni spoke of Chandu Baba as a truly great *siddha*.

The non-commercial saints of India are often unknown outside a local grouping. They tend to be an elusive minority, and attempts of the investigator to seek them out are fraught with difficulty to say the least, since they are averse to such spotlight as much as the fakes seek to attract it. The modern enthusiast who takes to the road (or stays at home) is likely to glorify a near or complete bogus who satisfies him on the basis of externals. It is very easy for some to be convinced that they have found "the real thing." In the process, the genuine article might well be bypassed with complete disdain or total non-recognition.

After an eventful stay, on 4th August 1916 Upasni Maharaj left Kharagpur without informing anyone. Sufi projects may be relatively short in duration if the inner objective has been achieved – or they may continue in another form. His aim was not to be a social reformer. In terms of social statistics, Kharagpur, or even the Monghyr district, was a drop in the ocean; at that time nobody could hope to do more than point to the necessary redress on a national scale. There were other outstanding individuals who could fill the reforming role at political level, notably Gandhi, who was soon to take up the task in earnest.

The completed human (*insan-i-kamil*) will work in response to dominant needs that he can register through the medium of expanded awareness. These needs may change very frequently, and attunement to them baffles the strictly linear attitude of "create something once, then keep it going forever."

From Bengal he travelled south to the Central Provinces, his destination being Nagpur. Here was the home of his pupil Dr. Pillai, who had since journeyed back from Shirdi. Upasni stayed with this man for a short while; there is no record of any contact with Tajuddin Baba, who was then established in his colony at Waki. Anxious devotees in Kharagpur ascertained his whereabouts by wire through Chinnaswami; the adept had not disclosed his movements in advance for the obvious reason that hordes of admirers would have encumbered his exit.

He continued his habit of going about naked. Yet the city of Nagpur had recently become subject to stringent rules of modesty owing to British intervention, contrary to the more free and easy approach prevalent in the northern cities. The ambassadors of Edwardian England still could not understand a people who were not partial to cumbrous apparel (whether or not they could afford it), and the memsahibs in particular were apt to get hysterical at nakedness, whether it was holy man or beggar that was the offender. It didn't happen in London, so why should it happen here? Would not these horrible Hindu ascetics look so much better if they were converted and wore nice tweed suits and white collars? The parson in his Sunday best was so much more respectable, they thought. It does not seem to have occurred very much to the critics that India was a very hot country, and that many of its inhabitants had no money, or even materials, for clothing. The inhabitants of the poorer villages could muster only the barest rags, which had a sad habit of wearing out.

It therefore happened that a police officer accosted Upasni under the orders of his superior, telling him to wear some clothes, since walking naked in the streets of Nagpur was forbidden, and he was transgressing the law.

In reply to this official visitation, Upasni simply asked the police officer whether he (Upasni) looked naked to him. It is said that the officer then saw that the accused was wearing a smart *pitamber* (a silk cloth with a golden border) in sudden contrast to his former nakedness. If it was an optical illusion, it seems to have been shared by hundreds of other citizens, who after the policeman's hasty departure, expressed their devotional enthusiasm by carrying Upasni in triumph (wearing the *pitamber*) through the streets.

This episode might be construed as an example in action of a sufi principle elsewhere expressed as: "When in Rome, do as the Romans do." The resulting public recognition seems to have become a little overpowering however, and he quickly moved on to Shindi, there to stay once more with Dr. Ganapatrao.

After another brief interval, he travelled back to Shirdi, where he settled himself once more in the outlying Khandoba's temple. His original pupils now had their opportunity to associate with him again. Things were different this time however; for one thing, news of his fame in the distant Kharagpur area had arrived ahead of him, and a large proportion of the visitors who came for the *darshan* of Sai Baba also went to seek out the occupant of the temple.

Striking a note of departure from Sai Baba's ways, he gave discourses that were understandable in terms of traditional Hindu doctrine, though with a directness that avoided mere repetition of Vedantic concepts. These discourses exerted a powerful appeal; during one of them, a large gathering remained attentive despite being fully exposed to the hot sun for a substantial period, still refusing to disperse even when an unexpected downpour of rain drenched the clothes of everyone present.

This eloquence was accompanied by some stronger medicine however. Though in some ways he catered for intellectual appetites, in other respects he furthered the "shock" attributes of his master, and to a more pronounced extent. He repeatedly discouraged the adulation that was beginning to accrue to him, and was quite capable of sending undesirables away from his discourse sessions. He was in fact liable to be openly ferocious if the situation demanded.

At nearby Shirdi one day, a certain ochre-robed swami happened to be sitting near Sai Baba. With an obvious air of equality, he asked the sufi about his health. It was clear that his assumed role of "spiritual" discipline and scriptural exposition had gone to his head, a shortcoming of many both in the East and West who read, write and teach subjects in which they are out of their depth. Like our swami, there are many who are liable to feel on equal footing with the genuine adept simply because they are accustomed to receiving the plaudits of the ignorant who take them at face value.

In reply to the obnoxious enquiry, Sai Baba said smoothly: "Yes, my health is alright. Go to Vithoba's temple and bring four hundred rupees." Putting two and two together, the swami asked again, "Shall I bring them from Upasni Maharaj?" Sai Baba answered amenably: "Yes, go! Bring them soon." The inflated visitor made his way with suitable decorum to the stipulated site, where he found Upasni sitting outside the temple in the shade of a banyan tree. In a voice of authority, almost of disdain, the newcomer accosted Upasni with the statement: "Baba has asked me to bring from you four hundred rupees. So I have come to demand them from you."

Upasni responded by administering a sound thrashing to the supercilious monk, handling him with both a strength and strategy that made the victim look like a naughty child. Pride received more injury than anatomy. After the beating, Upasni unceremoniously dismissed the swami with the words, "Have you now received your four hundred rupees?"

Returning to the mosque, the offended messenger related to Sai Baba what had happened, and the sufi coolly remarked: "He may not have given four hundred rupees to me, but it is a good thing that he has given them to you."

The conceited go-between then asked incredulously: "Did you send me there to receive a thrashing?"

Sai Baba replied laconically: "Sometimes a thrashing should also be received. What is the use of having only good things every day? I used to receive much thrashing."

There were several other occasions when Sai Baba sent similar individuals like this pompous swami to the abode of his chargeman. They usually received exactly the same form of manhandling. The remedy was effective enough, since the egos concerned, temporarily at least, lost wind to their sails.

Sai Baba had now only two more years of life, and had weakened a great deal in body. He could no longer give the same physical demonstrations as of old, but his fiery disciple could. Though past his prime at forty-seven years of age,

Upasni for long afterwards retained and expressed a bull-like energy that was apt to be strong stuff for those who liked to subsist upon a sugary sanctity.

Despite the increasing importance of Upasni Maharaj in the minds of visitors in general, the hard core of narrow-minded Shirdi devotees chose to view him merely as a rival of Sai Baba. This contingent were those who shouted loudest in the personality veneration of Sai Baba. They resented any inference that Upasni was the successor, blinding themselves to the issue by their one-track thinking. They were largely Hindus and not Muslims, be it noted, and so had no ground of complaint in terms of religious identity. These jealous supporters tried to make trouble for the new teacher, sometimes openly and at other times secretively. Sai Baba did not prevent this, since it was not necessary to do so. Those with sufficient perception were well aware of Upasni's importance; the others regrettably belonged to that devotional category who use up all their aspirational fuel on a single figurehead, and who prevent themselves from going any further when the opportunity presents itself. It was because of their antagonism that all reference to Upasni Maharaj was carefully avoided in later reports of the Hinduized Sai Baba, heavily implemented by Narasimhaswami's hurt pride.

It was not long before Upasni removed himself from this poisoned environment. He was also once again suffering from haemorroids, making another operation seem desirable. One of his pupils from the medical contingent was in contact with a good surgeon at Miraj, some distance south. Upasni consented to go there for treatment, but would not depart until someone obtained him permission from Sai Baba. He continued to acknowledge Sai Baba's authority in all things.

Upasni left Shirdi after a stay of about three months. This probably occurred in early 1917. He did not return again to his teacher's periphery.

CHAPTER FOUR

THE GREATER WORK

The operation was successfully carried out at Miraj, and subsequently Upasni travelled from place to place until he settled at Sakori in July 1917. This small village was only a few miles south of Shirdi. A local man named Shankar Patel wanted him to choose this rural location as a permanent residence. Upasni consented to visit Sakori, and consented to stay there, but his actual choice of abode was not an expected one.

Outside the village was a burial-ground, a desolate place bordered by open fields. It was here that Upasni said he wished to live, and so Patel and some of his neighbours obligingly built a small and simple hut for him at a spot indicated. It was the kind of lonely site relished by the more genuine ascetics, but was not for long to remain in such splendid isolation.

Nearby stood a large and solitary banyan tree, beneath which Upasni would frequently sit, sometimes discoursing, sometimes silent. His various pupils visited him, together with newcomers. The nearest railway station was Chitali, about nine miles away. The numbers grew rapidly, and a core of regular visitors emerged. Being a Hindu, he was largely to work with Hindus. The majority of his pupils were brahmins, on the whole erudite and partial to ritualism. There were a few Parsis like Gustadji Hansotia. Muslims were a comparative rarity, since Upasni concentrated upon a particular culture pattern.

The brahmin majority were attracted intellectually by Upasni's discourses on Vedantic themes. Their propensity for ceremony was likewise well to the fore, but this he clamped down upon from the start. However, he did take into account this conditioning factor by allowing those concerned to express the traditional ritualism in religious festivals that were held at Sakori. There were two of these prior to the death of Sai Baba in October 1918, each one lasting a full week. The next such festival was marked by an insistent urge for devotional ceremony on a more regular basis. Upasni was not favourable to this, holding that it had nothing to do with Advaita (non-dualism) and was a debasement of real *bhakti*.

One of those comparative few at Shirdi who transferred their attention to Upasni after the death of Sai Baba was a brahmin devotee named Bapusaheb Jog. He was an enthusiastic ritualist, being regarded as something of a specialist in this department, and had frequently been the leading figure in the *arati* performance before Sai Baba. Unlike other devotees at Shirdi who tried to mummify the past, Jog attached himself to the new current now in operation only a few miles away. He brought his *arati* fixation with him, but found that Upasni was not amenable to the idea of personal worship, as many other Hindus had also discovered.

After the third festival at Sakori, Upasni made a small concession to the ritualist element by allowing them to erect a small temple near his hut. Two photographs were placed inside, one of Sai Baba and the other of Maharaj. They could perform their worship before his picture, and that was all. To press him further was likely to risk his anger, a formidable enough deterrent to keep them in check.

This very masculine specimen of guruhood was not the sort of "master" now well known in the West as the result of mass media advertising. To date Upasni has received very little exposure outside India, and during his lifetime he continually rebutted attempts to make him into a celebrity of the kind to which false attitudes are partial.

Tall and well-built, with muscular limbs, he ate very simple food but enough of it. He kept his greying hair and beard cropped short. He was certainly not an emaciated figure with long locks trailing to the ground in the more picturesque yogi style. Nor was he the more modern pot-bellied variety of guru anxious to imitate, or benefit from, the Western ways that had now gained ascendancy. At

Sakori he frequently went about naked, a trait of some sadhu types, but a fact which could traumatize Westernized minds who were growing accustomed to current British ideas of respectability. He did however compromise with more urban laws by attiring himself in a lengthy piece of gunny cloth when making visits elsewhere, sometimes wearing this sacking material in the form of a loin-cloth, and at other times draping it over one shoulder so that it covered his body. Furthering the anti-sophistication approach, he had a very disconcerting (not to say frequent) habit of sitting and lying down in places notable for dirt or filth.

There were even more disconcerting factors. He was highly explosive, frequently venting his displeasure. People could often see why he was severe with others, but were more surprised when it came to themselves. Overbearing or greedy visitors were perhaps a priority, but pupils who saw him regularly were certainly not exempt. Vituperation was a standard feature of his method, but was backed up on occasions by singular demonstrations of muscular prowess in the form of beatings, whether over his knee or no. He was careful not to break any bones, but he did leave bruises. The extent of these manhandlings varied, but were extremely severe insofar as self-esteem was concerned. One should hasten to add that he confined these confrontations to healthy males who were neither stripling boys nor senile old men.

These tactics successfully repelled many seekers of the saintly, or the exotic, or the miraculous. Those who are easily attracted by externals can also be easily repelled by them.

There were critics and others who did not like him; he just was not their idea of a guru, of a brahmin. Therefore he could not be what they needed, or rather wanted.

To such minds, it was far better to go to a teacher who had more estimation of one's worth, who made the path easy, who promised God-realization just around the corner (and many powers), where all was love and bliss.

The detractors could never understand the testimony of hundreds of pupils who established a closer contact with him, who saw and experienced this stately personality to be an effective blend of real love and power that was not afraid to dispense with the ideals of pseudo-spirituality.

It is said that he was an enigma to outsiders, and that his ways remained inscrutable to the casual investigator. He himself frequently repeated a phrase from the *Bhagavad-Gita* in which Krishna says: "As I veil myself through yoga-created *maya* (ignorance, illusion), I do not manifest to all."

Salient characteristics of this no-nonsense guru can be conveniently summarized as follows:

1) He refused to act in the accepted saintly manner, though his ascetic disposition sets him far apart from those commercial gurus who have promoted a fashionable hedonism.
2) He refused to teach everyone who came to him.
3) He refused to treat as important people who believed that they were important, whether socially or spiritually.
4) He refused to be the recipient of attempted flattery.

To flatter Upasni Maharaj with ulterior motives was, to use a blunt phrase, "asking for trouble." To flatter oneself was likely to court a more absolute disaster.

The Hindu critics of the Sakori master had no idea that they were witnessing (or rather hearing about at second-hand) something to which they had an important clue in their scriptures. It was all very well being hazily acquainted with the idea that the personal consciousness is composed of arrangements of mental impressions or *sanskaras*, but pre-occupation with ceremonial and other diversions had long since done away with recognition of all the implications. What exactly are *sanskaras*? How are they attenuated? What complexities are involved in creating new impressions? These were questions that were never seriously asked, since it seemed more important to argue which school of the Vedanta had priority, or which method of chanting one used for recitations, or what procedure of etiquette one followed in rituals.

Upasni resorted to his more demonstrative outbursts when his verbal teaching was of little use in making the direct impact necessary to change mental and emotional responses. The full pursuit of our subject's teaching might lead us to Meher Baba's clarifications of such terms as "subtle body" and "mental body." One might even tackle references to the "universal mind," a thought-breaker over which some are liable to wrangle forever in relation to the perennial question of: does a form of omniscience really exist or not? These are now popularized concepts in the hands of the so-called mystics who peddle thirdhand variants of them. There are people who interminably expound these and other subjects without so much as even seeing a ghost; it is rather like a surfeit of exotic confectionery for the armchair gourmet, combined with a peculiarly sustained indigestion. Everyone and anyone can now lecture about these matters, diagrammatize them, commercialize them, discuss them, distort them, play with them in fashionable "workshops," and even tie them up with spaceships. The more knowledgeable are likely to advise the rhetoricians to use their commonsense, and if that is lacking, then to shut up.

Upasni Maharaj fundamentally taught his pupils straight *advaita* and pure *bhakti*, imparted expansion to those who earned it and beat hell out of those who needed such treatment. He cannot be accused of being vague in his blows delivered to self-esteem.

According to Upasni's Zoroastrian disciple Meher Baba, the expressed anger of the former was concerned with the eradication of sanskaric deposits lodged in non-physical extensions of the human being, "mental" substance having an intimate relationship with the brain, the true "subconscious" and more besides. These deposits, created by the cause and effect process called life, are existing and palpable formations in a more fundamental sense than, e.g., hair, teeth, and nails, which we all have to look after. The average man can be told that he has a subconscious mind which tends to manipulate him in a very jumbled manner (though it may seem ordered on the surface), but he cannot come to grips with it in more than almost useless fragments at a time. But sufi adepts and sadgurus are said to be able to tackle the ingredients in the raw; the degree of capacity here is often limited only by the incapacity of the pupil to bear the attendant strains involved, which can be very acute when two or more conflicting formations are given treatment.

The field of impressions completely rules daily and sleeping consciousness, and effectively imprisons consciousness. Impressions work by a kind of rebound action which forms itself through the polarity of opposite forces, e.g., pleasure and pain, joy and despair. They are continually being expended through the gamut of experiences, a process which just as quickly forms new impressions, since no total balance of opposites is struck. Every type of *sanskara* theoretically needs to be balanced by an opposite in what amounts to a mathematically precise pattern of cancelling-out. This balance is virtually impossible in practice. A man on his own can never see enough of the pattern ruling him to achieve this end, and is likely to make blunders at every critical juncture.

This total equilibrium is an important aspect of what occurs in "realization," of an almost mythical significance in many cases which do not achieve it. This occurrence is said to totally destroy the fixity of the opposites which hold consciousness in thraldom. The process of cancelling out impressions requires a special "unwinding" process in which the subconscious is gradually refined in substance, a process which wears out cruder imprints of all kinds. This gradual disposal of constricting influences creates a growing capacity to register finer and finer areas of consciousness which the more dense *sanskaras* effectively obscure.

Since the ordinary field of impressions serves to relegate higher "mystical" states to the mythological realm of day-dreams, it is not straightforward to be able to imagine what it is like to be in command of the subconscious mind from minute to minute. It is even less likely that the state of a completed human (*insan-i-kamil*) can be adequately envisaged, in view of the implications that this state has no subconscious at all, having been freed from impressions of all kinds and replaced by a consciousness of ultimate reality. It seems that enthusiasts are liable to view the distinctions of the highest office of a "master" with something of a neanderthal attitude to the space-rocket. If the real work of an adept is with the mental-physical circuit of impressions which rule individuals, then it is conceivable that this connects up in a larger pattern series with the momentum of communities and nations.

Upasni's first major excursion from Sakori appears to have been a visit to Benares in North India. This sacred city on the banks of the Ganges has long been a focal point for devout pilgrims who flock in their thousands to bathe in the waters and offer worship in the many temples. In this major brahmin stronghold, Upasni seemed more concerned with the poorer pilgrims, and the brahmin pupils who accompanied him offered to donate a generous sum of money to charity funds. He expressed his approval, and for once seemed pleased to preside at a ceremonial rite in connection with the almsgiving. In typical brahmanical style, the event was accompanied by the recitation of various Sanskrit texts by forty learned pundits.

Upasni Maharaj was no imitator. In contrast to Sai Baba, he would never ask for money, not even indirectly. Furthermore, he would not accept it even when it was offered freely. All he would ever accept was food, which he was not above begging for in the mendicant manner. A noteworthy example of this attitude occurred upon his return from Benares, when his followers practically pleaded with him to be able to render him some financial service. He wanted nothing; any money could go to the poor. But since lavish funds had only just been donated elsewhere, they were now insistent upon doing something specifically for him. Finally, he compromised by allowing them to erect suitable buildings in the vicinity for the accommodation of the growing number of visitors. This development itself provided him with opportunities to further one of his favourite social emphases: the integration of brahmin and untouchable. He made people from both these factions work together on the new buildings, drawing in voluntary village labour. Women participated also, by no means a common occurrence in caste society.

The burial-ground thus became an ashram, a word which can mean anything from a small retreat to a large colony. A number of his pupils settled there with him, mainly brahmins. He allotted various routine duties, and to some gave meditation instruction to complement their mundane labour.

A strict disciplinarian, Upasni could be extremely exacting in the face of laziness or incomplete attention. He was liable to respond harshly to such failures. His own temperament and habits were undeniably austere, and he expected much from his pupils in this direction. He disliked elegance, and was averse to flambuoyant clothing and lifestyles – quite unlike his contemporary Narayan Maharaj. His severity did not, however, lessen the devotion and loyalty felt towards him by his followers, since there was an underlying stimulus that complemented his tough exterior.

At the end of 1922, he gave instructions to a carpenter to convert a portion of his hut into a diminutive cage with wooden bars. In this cell he had himself interned on 21st December, 1922. The obedient carpenter fitted the last few bars after Upasni had entered the structure. This cage was just sufficiently long enough to allow him to recline at full length. It had no door or window to allow exit, although he was visible through the apertures made by the struts. He gave no explanation of this recourse to anyone. His pupils were concerned at the hardships he took upon himself, and asked him to tell them the reason for it all. He would only say that it was the will of the Supreme Being. He asked them all to continue their usual routine, and to be hospitable to any who came to Sakori with a serious aim.

In his restrictive cell he attended to all daily necessities, including bathing operations using the bucket and soap method of rural India. Resident pupils passed him food and other essentials through the bars, and attempted to keep the interior as clean as they could. From this voluntary prison he gave a number of discourses, daily talks which were recorded and later published in a limited local edition.

This confinement was not an ascetic exercise of the usual kind, but a reflex manifestation of an activity applying to adepts. This activity might best be referred to as the "greater work," something which transcends the work of self-development applying to those struggling on the inner path. It frequently involves some form of privation for the participants, though not always so obvious as in this instance.

There is one rather amusing episode to relate concerning

this privation. One of the ashram residents was Bapusaheb Jog, earlier mentioned. He and other brahmins had never relinquished hope of adding to the limited ritualistic fare at Sakori. Jog was the boldest spokesman, and had often entreated Upasni on this matter, though the latter was equally persistent in his refusals. But some while after the sadguru had entered the cage, Jog and others felt braver than usual now that the lion was behind bars. Upasni often seemed remote from his surroundings, and therefore they thought that perhaps he would not mind so much now. So they performed the *arati* before him, a simple enough ceremony it is true, and in devotional eyes quite innocuous. The teacher did not rebuke them, though he perhaps viewed the episode as a symptom of a more serious malady which they mistakenly wished to perpetuate.

Though these brahmins did not know it, his work was changing in accordance with wider needs, and their own role likewise in relation to it. His attitude to the ritualists was now, in effect: give a man enough rope to hang himself. What he had told them so many times before, he was not going to repeat in the same way anymore.

After more than thirteen months of confinement, Upasni gave an order for the carpenter to prepare a window in the cage, and accordingly stepped out of his cell on January 31st, 1924. He soon went back inside however, as if for some final adjustment, and emerged again on February 12th, this time conclusively.

Soon after this he visited Shirdi for the first time since the passing of Sai Baba. Accompanied by a large group of pupils, he first made his way to Khandoba's temple, in the interior of which he sat for some while. He spoke to pupils of past events that had happened there concerning him. As he spoke, tears flowed from his eyes, an unusual phenomenon for him. A number of people from Shirdi approached and awarded him a warm welcome. They led him to the venerated mosque, where he sat on the steps outside. Local people crowded round and gave him the same acclamation they would once have offered his teacher, even singing the same *arati* song associated with Sai Baba. Afterwards, Upasni visited the shrine nearby where he bowed down to the tomb and even joined in singing the special hymn reserved for the shrine. He then toured several other places in the village associated with the departed sufi, afterwards leaving Shirdi. But on his way back to Sakori, he paused to sit under the banyan tree in front of Khandoba's temple, and again shed tears. The inhabitants of Shirdi were still following him, and watched in fascination, since he was not noted for such displays of emotion. He spent some while under this tree before returning to his ashram.

Though the Shirdi populace well remembered him and regarded him with respect, popular response had lost contact with the progression of the essential activity which he carried on in the wake of Sai Baba. The officiators at Shirdi had long ago decided that Sai Baba had no successor.

The new Sakori community was somewhat disconcerted to find Upasni now undergoing a regular series of protracted confinements. Though they were not cut off from him, things were not the same as in earlier years. During the intervals he mixed with the community and was more attentive to visitors, though with characteristic unpredictability. Another regular aspect of a new rhythm of activity made itself felt, namely visits to distant places. Perhaps his longest sojourn away was the one occurring in 1927 when he suffered from a severe attack of dysentery and moved to Nasik for medical reasons until the affliction subsided. It was a lengthy illness lasting four months, and during that time his pupils from Sakori and elsewhere visited him for continued instruction.

While he was staying at Nasik, an event occurred which symptomatically illustrates the reason for the increasing decline of the ashram community in his activities. Some of the more prominent brahmins came to the conclusion that his wooden cage had acquired too dilapidated an appearance. This was too lowly for an important man they thought; he must have something better, something more of a testimony to his greatness. So they pulled down the simple wooden affair, and in its stead constructed a new cage made of silver bars. His immediate reaction is difficult to ascertain, but it was conceivably a heated one.

More and more Upasni occupied himself with travels to

major cities like Hyderabad (Deccan), Bombay, Kolhapur, Indore (Central Provinces), and other places spread over a wide area. Doing his best to avoid public exposure, he supervised pupils in these far-flung places, giving events a wider social emphasis when it was effective.

These travels and sojourns can be compared to similar excursions on the part of Narayan Maharaj. These contemporaries were much closer than mere dating correspondences. Upasni had gained realization much later in life, and knew what it was to have been "thoroughly painted inside and outside" as his senior in years had once expressed it. They did not need to meet in order to communicate, but maintained a significant dual action of complementary roles, the one richly bedecked and invariably benign, the other ascetic and fierce to all appearances: the perfect *jamali-jalali* polarity as expressed in a Hindu setting. These two teachers, the cream of Hindu culture, were both alike in that they did their best to create the impression that they were not masters of the highest grade.

Between the two of them, they maintained a unique impact upon Hindu society from Benares to Bangalore until the Second World War.

These two figures were the Hindu equivalents to the nominally Islamic contributions of Hazrat Babajan and Tajuddin Baba, all of them contemporaries, though the Muslims were the first to depart from the world.

The brahmins of the Sakori ashram tended to regard affairs there as the major focus of Upasni's activities. It was another symptom of the shortsighted approach which afforded ritualism such prominent attention. Upasni now allowed freer rein to their conditioned demands; traditional religious expression was increasingly difficult to check as a consequence of the larger following that was accumulating. He permitted the construction of a large temple, but took the opportunity to insist that it be open to the depressed classes and to non-Hindus. On important days in the Hindu religious calendar, followers from all over the country would congregate here to participate in the customary festivals. A progamme of non-stop repetition of sacred names was maintained in this shrine; it was begun by a group of female devotees in the 1920's and was enthusiastically continued without break while Upasni was alive.

He himself never lent importance to religious tradition of the extroverted type. On the social level, his emphasis was assistance to the multitude of poor. His mystical teaching stressed a psychology running counter to formalism. "Pure *bhakti* is the most delicate thing in the world, and this is what God really wants, nothing else," he used to tell the ritualists. Devotion, be it noted, is not pure *bhakti*, but a lesser form of it.

Well-meaning devotees hankered after serving him personally as a kind of attendant, seeing to his daily needs or trying to impose some small comfort upon his ascetic lifestyle. He deterred this tendency however, saying: "The master is never keen about the service of his own person. What he appreciates most is the service a person renders to humanity, which is a manifestation of God. The significance of the religion of service is very deep, and unfathomable even to the yogis."

In this higher perspective of service, he was only partly referring to the aspect of social welfare work that most are familiar with. Over and above this are the teaching functions of varying grades, which are climaxed by the supreme service of the "greater work."

The indifference of Upasni Maharaj to visitor's opinions may yet become proverbial.

One of the most well known visitors who went to Sakori was Mahatma Gandhi, sometime prior to the latter's headline visit to Britain in 1931. Typically enough, Upasni made no attempt to maintain a good impression. He removed his gunny cloth as he so often did, and said to his guest roughly: "You may be a great man; what is that to me? Why have you come here?"

Gandhi interpreted the gesture of nakedness as something audacious, and felt shocked at such gruff treatment. He was puzzled, and could make nothing of Upasni, who did not seem to him a saintly man.

Not long afterwards, in 1931 Gandhi encountered a well known disciple of Upasni, namely Meher Baba, whose much gentler demeanour had a more soothing effect upon him. He felt that the Parsi was someone truly great, and could not understand it when the latter impressed upon him that Upasni was nothing less than a real master in the full sense of the word.

It is relevant here to draw attention to one particular feature of the differences between Upasni and Gandhi, at the time of this episode, that has tended to be overlooked. Gandhi doubtless became aware of Upasni's strong condemnation of caste attitudes, a condemnation which sometimes took a distinctively aggressive manifestation. At the time Gandhi went to Sakori, he was still a conservative insofar as caste norms were concerned, having made no radical departure from them. It was only later in Gandhi's life that he cut a firm tangent to caste strictures; Louis Fischer charts the approximate date of the changeover as (or by) 1932. In Upasni's eyes therefore, at the time of their meeting, Gandhi was still a caste supporter, and hence his stinging remarks.

While the brahmins at Sakori sought every excuse to maintain their favoured drill of onerous ceremonial, Upasni was known to comment, "I do not want this brahmin atmosphere of men."

Left to their own devices, these brahmins would have turned Sakori into one more temple complex of the sort with which India abounded. Most pupils of any teacher tend to do the equivalent in terms of the dominant collective background – whether ascetics, scholars, soldiers, devotees, shopkeepers, musicians, or priests.

Since he was largely concerned with Hindu culture, and because he became an influence upon a brahmin sector, Upasni had to take into account priestly conditioning patterns. But since he was Upasni Maharaj, he did not let the priests have it all their own way. Those who are liable to think that he set about changing events merely by foaming at the mouth, should know that the method which he adopted in this instance was far more subtle than a *jalali* tirade, and possibly more effective in the long term.

The untouchables were not the only oppressed sector in Hindu society. Women also tended to be the underdogs.

Though not restricted to the same degree of purdah as many urban Muslim women, and though they never suffered compulsory deformity of the feet as in China, Indian women were far from being free agents. Leaving out such extremes as the notorious *sati* (suttee) custom outlawed by the British, it is a fair enough summary to state that females in general had no choice in their course of life from early marriage to the extremely dour statutes governing widowhood. They had little chance of changing their fate, since they had absolutely no say in matters, a fact which sent the late nineteenth century reforming genius Vivekananda into virtual fits of mingled rage and despair at the automatism of his compatriots.

Upasni Maharaj, or Upasni Baba as he was sometimes known, likewise seems to have decided that this matter was due for remedy. From the start he had been extremely considerate of women, and had taken every opportunity to draw them into activities as unlikely as construction work, not in order to produce a new breed of amazons, but to ensure that they did not get left at the hearthside. A notable feature of his memorable manual labour at Kharagpur had been to assist poverty-stricken women in their daily round.

His early pupils could remember a strange phenomenon during his days of transition at Khandoba's temple. While undergoing the superhuman *fana-baqa* process, he had sometimes been observed to act as if he were a woman, something which had puzzled them, since Upasni was anything but effeminate.

It is to be noted that he was never the *jalali* tiger with women, only with men. Female pupils were prone to verbal rebuke however, like everyone else, since they were not egoless by virtue of their sex.

While Gandhi was increasingly spotlighting the plight of the Harijans (untouchables), Upasni Maharaj increasingly turned his attention to women, whom he favoured more than the brahmins. He began to gather together at Sakori a special contingent of young women and girls, carefully selecting them from various families. He began to specifically train them in a life that might be described as one of pure character and spiritual aspiration. They became a community of Hindu nuns. In the usual way, these women would have had no choice as to how they wanted to live, even if they could have formed a sufficient directive at an early age. Marriage to a partner selected for them would have been an automatic procedure. There were no official convents in India, and the common alternative was to become a mendicant – and there are not so many women as tough as Hazrat Babajan.

This group was a distinctly unusual feature of an Indian ashram at that date. Vivekananda had wished to establish a form of convent a generation before, but dull-minded resistance outwitted his short life-span, and it took a Westerner, his female disciple Margaret Noble (alias Sister Nivedita) of determined Celtic blood, to struggle to maintain a unique school for girls in Calcutta.

The female novices of Sakori were known as *kanyas*. Upasni did his best to ensure that they did not grow up with rigid religious notions, though he was very strict in his disciplinary requirements. The most promising girl in his judgment was one who became known as Godavri Mai, whose exceptional abilities gradually became evident. She had first come into contact with him as a child of ten in 1924. He had placed her upon his lap, and referring to the ashram around him, said to her inscrutably, "All this belongs to you."

Godavri was afterwards reared at the ashram, and Upasni frequently expressed a high estimation of her. This caused jealousy amongst some of the other female residents, who attempted to harass her in petty ways, and "did their best to break her" to use a realistic description of their attitude. They were hopelessly the losers in popularity stakes however. In his last years, Upasni was known to tell many visitors: "Do not bow to me, but worship her (Godavri)."

The brahmin elders looked upon all this with mixed feelings. On the one hand, they could not doubt that what Maharaj did was right, but he seemed to be giving this *kanya* community a priority attention. There was now a most alarming thought: an ashram dominated by women. It was enough to make nonsense of all their efficacious rites.

We are now moving well into the 1930's, and must pause

to give due mention to a newcomer upon the scene who is already known to the reader from Part One. Swami Narasimhaswami arrived hotfoot from Nasik, accounting himself to have been snubbed by one Meher Baba, who would not let him write his (Baba's) biography. Surely this Upasni Maharaj would think better of the proposal, or did none of these sages want their deeds proclaimed in print? Would he really need to trudge all the way up north to Rishikesh to find a willing candidate? As most Hindus are now aware, many of the gurus in tourist locations are not that advanced.

Narasimhaswami was deeply gratified to find that Upasni did not seem to mind him staying at Sakori with the brahmins there, and that he did not present any objection to having a biography compiled. Not that he actually encouraged the enterprise, but he did not veto it. Not like that Meher Baba who would not even let him stay at his ashram. No, Upasni Maharaj would now have the benefit of his literary services; it was Maharaj that would be extolled to the skies. Justice would win the day. Meher Baba was a Persian nonconformist anyway; far better to champion a good home-grown brahmin.

The biographer found that contact with Upasni Maharaj was highly stimulating, since one never knew what was going to happen next – though it was apt to be disconcerting if one happened to be on the receiving end of his displeasure. A difficult point this, but there were some really nice discourses – and more important than anything else, events which were obviously in the nature of miracles. Yes, he could make sense out of these marvellous occurrences, just waiting to be written up; this was the stuff of which great books were made. He did not care much for Upasni's close connection with the *kanya* community however. He, Swami Narasimhaswami, was a monk as the title implies, and he was made of sterner stuff than to mix with women.

Doggedly, our monkish writer kept at his notes, fitting the pieces together and rounding off apparent inconsistencies (to his way of thinking) as best he could. But he was proud of the final result, and was intent upon getting it published straightaway.

The author of the *Sage of Sakori* could not understand why Upasni did not seem grateful for the service rendered him. Surely he must be pleased now that everyone would know how great he was? But no, he seemed as rude and uncouth as ever. The elation of authorship was punctured, and Narasimhaswami set to thinking on different lines. Over and above the unsociable attitude, he now fastened upon the community of nuns. There was something wrong here, he thought; there was no precedent for such an arrangement. Had he made a mistake after all? What about the book he had just published? This might rebound upon his reputation if he was not careful. Upasni Maharaj did have rather a lot of detractors, and when all said and done, he was not really what many expected of a holy man.

In the last analysis, Swami Narasimhaswami thought like many other monks: if you have much to do with women, it is because you are amorously attracted to them – something to be abhorred, rather like having a guru who is married, or meditating without sitting crosslegged. Now Upasni clearly had a lot to do with these nuns, and some of them were really quite attractive to look at. More suspicious even, he seemed to prefer their company to that of the learned and devout brahmins.

His final conclusion was that Upasni could not be a master. Upasni was not spiritual enough.

It was such proscribing attitudes as this which had helped to keep Indian women in subjection for many centuries, possibly since the early Jainist and Buddhist era two and a half thousand years ago. In that very different age, Mahavira the Jain is reported to have admitted many thousands of women into his monastic order (far more women than men), an occurrence which may have been paralleled on a smaller scale by his younger contemporary Siddharta Gautama, known as the Buddha. Such ancient heretics may be said to have raised the social status of women through monastic channels. But one wonders how many limited ascetic mentalities viewed ascetic female groupings as disguised harems.

Swami Narasimhaswami set off down the road to Shirdi,

there to rescue his name from association with Upasni Maharaj by a new biographical venture. A rich field of unplumbed miracle material awaited him, unhindered by unusually fierce gurus and distracting communities of nuns.

While the Narasimhaswamis came and went, Upasni Maharaj did what had to be done with those who could respond correctly instead of toying for selfish ends. He was now well into his sixties. During his last few years of life he began to accept offerings of money for the first time, either using it for the ashram expenditure or donating it to the poor.

To the end he remained a man of fire, a human thunderbolt who shattered preconceptions in those who could bear to part with such flotsam. He now lived under a dual stigma applied by his detractors. Some said he was too ascetic, too extremist, too unsociable. Others said he was not ascetic enough, not holy enough. Both views were in agreement that he was not the ideal guru.

As might be expected, Upasni Maharaj went out with a bang. There was to be nothing tame for him, no sedate course to *mahasamadhi* of the type depicted in standard hagiographies.

The giant who had been surrounded by pygmy mentalities for the past quarter-century, was now to give them something to think about that they would not forget in a hurry (though whether such memory has been accurately functioning is another matter).

It began when hidebound Hindu paters began to intervene in the lives of the *kanya* community. In the traditional view, marriage was the only legitimate course for a woman; for one thing, a woman was economically useless, and it was a key objective to team up a hapless daughter with a promising son-in-law. That was her function more or less. If one did not marry her off as quickly as possible, one risked a financial liability, longstanding worries, and conventional disapproval. No matter if the woman was exceptionally intelligent, or disliked her selected partner, or got the worst end of the deal in other ways; these were absolutely immaterial factors to the social machine. Women were born to marry and rear children, and that was that. It was unfortunate if their husbands died, because they could not marry again, and many had to live in penury in addition to perpetual mourning (in the old days of course, some of them went on the funeral pyre). Solution: avoid getting born as a woman in your next incarnation.

These unreasoning paters stepped on the tiger's tail, and the resulting roar of anti-bigotry shook the social code. This time Upasni did not give way to orthodoxy an inch; he had allowed rituals, but he would not allow the attempted abduction of *kanyas* (nuns). Many times during previous generations, young women who had wanted to stay at places like ashrams had been pressed into unwanted matrimony, in which direction unwillingness was a punishable matter in the family eye.

Upasni Maharaj dared to do what lesser men would never have contemplated. He quickly arranged a marriage between himself and one of the threatened women, and then another, and then another. At the age of sixty-eight, he took six wives. His stunned brahmin pupils temporarily forgot their rituals, while the paternal representatives went wild with indignation at this sidestepping of custom. Upasni was old, and had not a penny to his name. It seems also that the interferers were urged on by the malevolent gossip of his "holier than thou" detractors. The episode was dubbed a scandal in caste circles.

Upasni was issued with a legal summons to appear in court at Ahmednagar. He duly appeared before the judge and jury, clad in his simple gunny cloth. The case was protracted, but the upshot was that his wives were saved from an unwanted fate. Monogamy had not been legalized in India, and the British had enough other troubles on their hands at that time.

The total repercussions and implications of the event can be listed as follows:

(a) His purpose in aiding six women and in keeping intact the community of nuns is obvious.

(b) His brahmin followers were shocked into a deeper cognizance of events, and were forced into acknowledgment of the role of the selected women at Sakori.

(c) The episode served as a "malamati" (to use a sufi term) technique inviting opprobrium. His detractors crowed loudly, for in their estimation, a holy man getting married was like losing caste. Calumnies were heaped upon him, and from now on visitors were largely in abeyance, miracle mongers and all. The average guru would not have dared to court such public disapproval, in those days before the advent of publicity measures attendant upon the Californian boom in decadent gurus.

(d) He was drawing attention, in the most concrete manner, to a serious social discrepancy, for any witnesses who were not blinkered enough to look askance.

Six wives was also the quota of the Prophet Muhammad (who could boast nine in all), who has always been a subject of opprobrium for pious monogamists, despite the fact that he was possibly the greatest sociological genius of the Middle Ages. Amongst other things, Muhammad effectively limited the number of Arab wives to four per man, whereas previously an unlimited number was permissible. Only the more aristocratic members of Islam exceeded his statutes, notably the tenth century sufi exponent Ibn Khafif of Shiraz, who is reported (probably with some exaggeration) to have contracted four hundred marriages. The latter's example should not be confused with the later Sultans of Turkey however, since the Iranian patriarch is reported to have remained strictly celibate outside his first partnership.

In many ways, Upasni Maharaj was in advance of his times. It was not until the mid-1950's that the government of Jawaharlal Nehru was able to introduce new laws for the benefit of women. There was considerable obstruction to these laws even amongst Congress members, and the revision programme was not complete for some years afterwards.

Upasni Maharaj had not quite finished with the world. After proving how sociable he really was, he played his last ace for those who must have some renunciate code to prove that spirituality exists.

He did not set up home with his new wives; they were merely part of his unique community of female pupils. He remained strictly celibate, and after the fuss had died down a little, he commenced a final demonstration in the more exacting ascetic mode.

Having long ago dispensed with the exotic cage provided by the brahmins, he now confined himself in a new cage made of bamboo sticks. Not usually being one to do things by halves, he had specified that this cell be limited to measurements of only three feet by three and a half feet. This meant that he was not able to lie down in it, which amounted to a chronic discomfort at seventy years of age. Evidently by his standards, to make it any bigger would have been cheating.

This last confinement commenced about mid-October 1940, and save for rare occasions when he briefly emerged for important matters, he remained in the cage night and day until December 1941. During these fourteen months, he maintained an extremely severe fast on coffee only. He naturally became somewhat lean in appearance. Though not in the best of health, there still seemed abundant vitality in him. In case anyone might imagine compensating gallons of coffee being daily consumed by the cage occupant, it should be noted that he limited himself to a moderate quantity of this liquid taken only once each twenty-four hours.

On December 22nd 1941 he left Sakori for his birthplace Satana, giving the impression that he would remain there until the end of the month. But he returned the next day owing to illness. In the early hours of the 24th, he complained of a pain in the heart. His pupils resorted to the usual domestic remedies, and a mustard-plaster was applied to his chest. Resting upon a couch, he assured everyone that he would be free from pain in a few minutes. Not wishing to disturb him, his attendants left him alone for two or three hours. They noticed that he never moved once, not even to change sides. They began to feel uneasy, and called for the other residents of the ashram. The doctor was hurriedly called for, arriving about an hour later from Kopargaon. He soon declared to the anxious onlookers that life had been extinct in the patient for some hours.

This sudden, unobtrusive death took everyone completely by surprise.

Godavri Mai, outstanding amongst the community of nuns, was subsequently recognized as the head of the ashram. Matters went in advance of long past events at nearby Shirdi, since a resident successor to the guru was acknowledged. It was a very unusual feature for a female to be so honoured.

It had been obvious that Upasni had wished for his young disciple Godavri to take charge of Sakori after his death, though he had other important disciples elsewhere. Such extensions fall outside the scope of this book. Insofar as Sakori was concerned, Godavri Mai's convent community continued, and each woman spent a number of years as a novice before gaining the insignia of a yellow sari.

Rich brahmin devotees erected lavish buildings around the shrine (*samadhi*) of Upasni. Sakori today bears no resemblance to the stark place of the dead where Upasni Maharaj took up residence during the First World War.

Bibliography:

The best source in English is that by Dr. Chakradar D. Deshmukh of Nagpur University, whose biogaphy of Upasni appeared in *The Meher Baba Journal* (Ahmednagar-Bangalore, 1938–42), and was reprinted in *The Awakener* (New York, 1965). Also useful is the shorter account by C.B. Purdom in *The Perfect Master* (London, 1937), pp. 27 ff. An earlier biography than Narasimha-swami's mixed offering was written by two Muslims, Dr. Abdul Ghani Munsiff and S.A. Abbas Khak. This was in Urdu, and entitled *Garibonka Asra* (Protector of the Poor). Also published in the 1920's was a Marathi biography by Nath Mahadeo, a famous novelist of the time. The Parsi writer Sorabji M. Desai wrote a biography in Gujerati, also at the request of Meher Baba during the 1920's. Meher Baba's quotation at the end of my chapter two comes from D.E. Stevens, *Listen Humanity* (New York: Dodd, Mead and Co., 1957), p. 64. A brief account in English was included in Mani Sahukar, *Sai Baba: The Saint of Shirdi* (third edn, Bombay 1983), one of the very few reports of Sai Baba to give Upasni recognition.

On the Vedantic background, see Part Three of my *Minds and Sociocultures* (forthcoming). On Godavri Mai, see Mani Sahukar, *Sweetness and Light: Life and Teachings of Sati Godavari Mataji* (Bombay, 1966). The present author has written a brief unpublished biography of Narayan Maharaj. On Gandhi and caste, see Louis Fischer, *The Life of Mahatma Gandhi* (1951; repr., London: Granada, 1982), pp. 419–20. On Gandhi and Upasni, see C.B. Purdom, *The God-Man* (London, 1964), p. 95. Rare information on Upasni's later marriages comes from the late Adi K. Irani, a Parsi who knew Upasni personally and whose mother Gulmai was one of his oldest disciples of the Sakori phase; the relevant reminiscences appeared in *The Glow* (Bombay, 1977), from talks given in London in 1976. Details of Upasni's death were reported very close to the time of occurrence in *The Meher Baba Jnl* by F.H. Dadachanji, another Parsi.

Upasni was subject to a distorted cameo portrait in Paul Brunton, *A Search in Secret India* (London: Rider, 1934; second edn, 1970), pp. 56, 63. Brunton, alias H. Raphael Hirsch, was a journalist who never met Upasni and who reported hearsay in this unreliable bestseller. He says that a Parsi named Khandalawalla, a former Judge of Bombay, debunked Upasni as having made "ghastly mistakes" like telling his (Khandalawalla's) son-in-law that his speculations on the Bombay Stock Exchange would prove extremely fortunate for him. This son-in-law lost capital as it transpired, and the affluent Khandalawalla was evidently unable to digest the implications that spirituality is not equivalent to vast resources of material wealth. It should be added that Khandalawalla was also biased against Upasni owing to the latter's association with the Parsi ascetic Meher Baba, who was not in favour with some orthodox Parsis. On the dubious nature of Brunton's report of Meher Baba, see the relevant chapter in my *Meher Baba, an Iranian Liberal* (forthcoming), which is a sociological and philosophical study. Since most Western readers only know Upasni through such a hearsay reporter as Brunton, it seemed incumbent in the present book to rectify the bias by a more sympathetic treatment. Upasni was exceptional for his social policies, and though certain of his traits are offputting to some religionists, he deserves a much stronger profile than has formerly been awarded him. The commercial jingoism of Brunton was unconcerned with policies of social amelioration and the correction of crass tendencies. "Secret India" did not divulge its true wealth.

Former sympathetic treatments of Upasni did not adequately integrate the various levels of content. Deshmukh's report abovementioned gave much factual information, but is lacking in some important details of Upasni's last years. Purdom's account was too brief to bring out finer points. On the basis of the factual data, Upasni emerges as a remarkably independent entity whose like is not easily found in latter day reports of gurus. A comparison with Swami Vivekananda is apt in some respects, though there are some differences. Upasni seems to have taught approximately the same philosophy as Ramana Maharshi, though his temperament was very different. The dual ascetic and domestic features in Upasni's life pattern invite a necessarily qualified description in terms of a Vedantic version of a non-sensual tantric affinity. I have developed variants of this theme in my annotated introduction to *Vivekananda: his life and teaching* (in preparation). Cf. Mircea Eliade, *Yoga: Immortality and Freedom* (London: Routledge & Kegan Paul, 1958).

Upasni's asceticism was formidable by any standards. Though I have never seen it stated in any account of him, it is evident that his last fast must have medically contributed to his decease. It seems that he wanted to prove that the ideal is never compromised by those who have achieved it, whatever the outward appearances.

About the Author:
Kevin R.D. Shepherd was born in 1950, and has been engaged in an extensive private research project since 1977. He is the founder of the Intercultural Research Centre of Anthropography, a non-political educational project which was initiated in November 1984 upon completion of his manuscript *Meaning in Anthropos: Anthropography as an interdisciplinary science of culture*, which now awaits publication. Anthropography is a new science of culture conceived and promoted by the author in a polymathic sense of commitment.

Anthropography covers philosophy, the social sciences, the human sciences, natural science, and the history of religions. It is both scientific and humanistic. Anthropography here extends well beyond current dictionary definitions; the geographical distribution of mankind is given a polymathic focus that does not obscure intrinsic evolutionary dimensions.

Anthropography does not stress mere polymathy as an antidote to over-specialized studies, but is concerned to indicate the priorities that should govern a comprehensive curriculum.

The interdisciplinary strategy of anthropography takes particular account of the heritages of non-Western peoples. The European heritage is also covered, but not at the expense of Asiatic contributions. The author is currently working upon a series of books which has a cross-cultural relevance to Western, Islamic, Jewish, Indian, Chinese, and other culture-groups.

His first book *Psychology in Science* (Cambridge, 1983) was an unusually forthright essay incorporating a support for the ecological and interdisciplinary emphases of the Club of Rome, and a critique of scientific materialism and relativism. He defines himself as being primarily a philosopher, a stance readily apparent in his *The Resurrection of Philosophy*, which similarly awaits publication.